Becoming Lovers

The Journey

From Disciple of Christ to Bride of Christ

Becoming Lovers

The Journey from Disciple of Christ to Bride of Christ

Book cover and layout designed by
John Centofanti, Creative Stream Marketing
www.CreativeStreamMarketing.com

Cover photo courtesy of
Ali Taylor, London, England
www.AliTaylorPhotography.co.uk

ISBN: 978-1-886296-44-2

Dedication

I dedicate my life to my savior, ***Jesus Christ.*** I thank Him for entrusting me with the message of this book. I take no credit for it, only the responsibility to remain committed to live up to its truth and encourage others to do the same.

I am, however, gratefully indebted to one man for helping me to learn what has become this book. And so, I dedicate this project to my husband,

Perry James Chickonoski.

It has been his unfailing love, first and most importantly to God, and secondly to me and our children, that has made all that I have been taught come alive.

I am most grateful to God for bringing him into my life and hope that every Christian woman could have a husband willing to be used by God to do the same for them.

I also lovingly thank my parents, ***Jim and Georgia Leone,*** for their faithful example of authentic Christianity. My Father has served God as a pastor most of my life with my mother faithfully beside him all the way. Through every storm, some of which I created, they have been obedient to God without wavering. Thank you, Dad, for your kind and wise words in the foreword of this book. My parents have been a vital and irreplaceable part of my Christian growth and experience with God. If it were not for them, I would not be writing this at all.

A big thanks goes out to all the people who helped me finish this project: My children ***Carley, Cami and Perry*** for giving up some of their time with mom, so I can dedicate myself to God's work; Gina Biondello, editing; John Centofanti, layout and cover design; Arrow publications; Teri Moser promotions; and Jim Leone, publicity.

Finally, thank you, the reader, for taking an interest in this book. May God bless you as abundantly for reading it, as He has me for penning it.

Contents

Foreword

As I considered the foreword of this book, I was reminded of a previous conversation I had years ago. I was in a pre-conference leadership meeting for Promise Keepers in Boulder, Colorado. The guest speaker was speaking on "A Man's Starting Place." He had been a mentor of mine via media, books and conferences. In speaking with him, I asked the question, "What are the things that will make a difference in my life in the next five years?"

His answer was very simple, "The books you read and the relationships you establish will make all the difference." So, I asked him what books he would suggest. What he said was something I will never forget, "Unfortunately, most people will select a book that tells them what they want to hear, what they already know and agree with. Yet, learning is not the consequence of teaching, writing, or reading, but thinking. A book that is challenging, unclear to you, stimulating, and causes you *to* think, not *what* to think, is more worthwhile." Joy, in this book, has certainly done that–she causes her reader to think.

I personally believe that every one of us needs a book like this, where we can be on an adventure, involved in a story and launched on a journey with direction. Our Creator Himself yearns to be involved with each of us personally and intimately. He wants us to hear His voice leading us, loving us, and empowering us in the midst of the challenges we face in life.

When our hearts are at a loss for words, and schedules crowd out our time with God, this book gives us practical ways to approach our personal relationship with Jesus. The Holy Spirit has filled Joy's heart with creativity; enabling us to overcome life's obstacles with a new perspective. Joy shares her ideas with us and encourages us to be interactive in each chapter.

Several virtues of the book are particularly significant in our pursuit of spiritual formation. First, the book maintains focus on God, our Creator, and

Jesus Christ as the center of our spiritual life. Secondly, Joy surveys ways in which God draws us into relationship with Himself. Finally, the tone of the book is honest, authentic and self-critical.

In Joy's discussion of rejection, criticism, and the part they play in our pursuit of God, she makes this statement about the modern church, "Abundant life has a tendency to mean the American dream, but abundant life is the ability to live with hope, grace and love in spite of difficulties." May we all live the abundant life.

I am thrilled for all this book will mean to people like you and me. Readers from all over will have their lives invigorated, their purpose will be transformed, and they will impact the missional church and the post-modern world around us.

Pastor Jim Leone
Youngstown, Ohio

Words of Endorsement

This is really a wonderful book, both in content and layout. I'm excited about what the Lord will do with this powerful resource.

Francis Frangipane
Pastor, River of Life Ministries
Frangipane Ministries, Inc.
Cedar Rapids, IA

To know Joy Chickonoski is to know someone who understands the difference between obeying rules, being religious, and having a living, breathing, vibrant relationship with God!

In "Becoming Lovers," she draws out of her own walk with the Savior as well as her observations and revelations on the journey, which as she states, is the destination.

Rather than offering some "quick fix" for what ails you spiritually, Joy's goal is to create a greater hunger and thirst for intimacy with the King.

You will be challenged, and I believe changed, as you take this journey from being a disciple of Christ to bride of Christ!

David L. Thomas
Pastor, Victory Christian Center
Founder & Director, NxL Network
Lowellville, OH

Joy's blend of biblical insight and life experience cause this work to be fresh and thought-provoking. Her desire for intimacy with God bleeds through the pages of her writing.

Pastor Tony LaGamba, Pastor
High Pointe Assembly of God
Poland, Ohio

Joy has always demonstrated a deep love for the Lord and His Word. Her experiences in life and ministry give her unique credentials from which to write. I am confident that you will be challenged to grow spiritually and motivated to reach your divine potential as you read her work.

Doug Clay, District Superintendant
Ohio District Council of the Assemblies of God
Columbus, Ohio

The Beginning... it just keeps going when the journey is eternal.

We are always at the beginning with God, because the journey never ends. We are always a novice no matter how long we have walked with God. To be ignorant of this truth is to walk with a small God.

Our God is an awesome God

The beauty of God's salvation is astounding to me. I marvel at the wisdom of God every time I see His signature in creation. Like the colors of a sunset so bright and vibrant, yet never have I seen the same sunset twice. Pondering creation has taught me a lot about the character and personality of our heavenly Father.

Surely, a God who creates sunsets is fun and lively, not boring and rigid like so many see Him. The first time I held my firstborn daughter and felt her soft skin against mine, I knew that God loved me more than I would ever know in this life time. I have been overwhelmed by the goodness of God every time I look into my husband's warm brown eyes and see his adoration and love for me shining through. Just to know that God has chosen me to be His is both empowering and humbling.

I am no longer satisfied to just say I am saved; I need to proclaim it to the world. I demonstrate this passion in worship as I dance before God, allowing my whole body to tell the story of God's amazing love. I declare my allegiance to Jesus in the life that I live through Him. I desperately want to please God with the choices I make and the things that I do, say, and think. I have this desire because I have been captivated by the love of God, and that great love compels me.

Many people are motivated to be a Christian by fear or family tradition; this falls so short of what our heavenly Father desires for us. I want people to know the real God who loves them passionately. I pray that my life will be a testimony of God's truth to others. I try to portray God's love every time I see someone in need and realize that God is giving me the chance to touch his or her life with His beauty.

I have experienced God's beauty, both in His blessings and His loving discipline. God desires to unfold His true nature to us; in the good and the bad, the easy and the hard, the things asked for and the things we dread. God is both power and love at the same time. His fierce holiness commands our allegiance and His selfless love melts our hearts. It is an extraordinary experience to see the perfection of both of these attributes working in harmony. When our goal in life is to see God, life takes on a new meaning. We no longer have to fear the unknown or the unwanted. Instead, we can say like the woman of Song of Solomon, "Awake, north wind and come south wind blow on my garden that its fragrance may spread abroad..." (Song of Solomon 4:16).

This woman no longer feared blessing (south wind) as though embracing it would bring hardship. She also welcomed difficulty (north wind), knowing her submission to God's will would bring greater revelation into her life. This place of surrender brings freedom and safety that no human element of control could ever duplicate. It is truly beautiful.

Each chapter will unfold the stages, struggles and surprises of pursuing Jesus passionately.

I am captivated by Jesus. The more I know Him and understand Him the more His beauty compels me to follow him no matter the cost. I have asked the Holy Spirit to impart to you what I have seen and learned along my journey with our heavenly Bridegroom. My earnest prayer for you is that, through this book, you will experience the touch of God that will lead you into a more intimate relationship with Jesus. My challenge to you is to go deeper, reach higher and never settle for anything less than the Father's dreams for you. Our God is an awesome God!

Trusting in the Sovereignty of God

This book will describe the journey of a true Christian. Each chapter will unfold the stages, struggles and surprises of pursuing Jesus Christ passionately. For some of you the first several Chapters may be a reflection back to an earlier time in your Christian journey. Do not just breeze through these chapters, sometimes God's gentle reminders can be the sweetest times in His presence.

It is not my intention to formulate your theology; although some things discussed in this book may cause you to reevaluate your theological beliefs. Instead, my goal is to challenge and motivate you to seek a more intimate walk with Jesus Christ. I am certain that along the way, if not already, I will say things that you may view differently.

I encourage you to take these things to the Lord, rather than overlook them. God loves it when we give him the opportunity to reveal something new to us. If at any time while reading this book you feel strong emotion, negative or positive, please close the book and go to God. I firmly believe, contrary to some religious teaching, that God does want us to be emotional. The Father does not want you to quench, suppress or ignore your emotions; instead he wants you to use them. Use your emotions as you would the *check engine* light on your car dash. If the warning light comes on, you do not ignore it or smash it so it does not work any more. You use that light as an indication that something should be examined.

Use your emotions in the same way. They can be an indication to you that God needs to examine something in your heart or reveal something that is in His heart. Go to God when this happens. The Father longs to speak to you. He is waiting to show Himself to you in a new way. What a privilege our relationship with God is; do not neglect it.

I want to encourage you to meditate on this book, do not just read it. For this purpose, you will notice large margins. This will give you, the reader, a place to record your thoughts and commentary. Then you can return to these writings for closer evaluation and study.

I have also created special sections called "Soul Soaks" in order to help you to meditate. Just to clarify, meditation is a biblical experience that the new age movement has redefined. The New Age form of meditation means to empty your mind. This is dangerous because you become susceptible to suggestion, which the devil uses to his advantage. However, the biblical form of meditation means to fill your mind with God's truth.

To biblically meditate on this book means to take what you read to the Lord; then He can speak to your heart concerning His truth I have presented. The Soul Soak is a way to meditate, letting your soul soak up all that God has for you to experience. "SOAK" is an acronym for:

S Still your mind so you can discern God's voice over your own or others.

O Open your heart to new revelation from the Holy Spirit.

A Affirm God's truth when the Holy Spirit brings conviction or insight.

K Kindle new passion for Jesus by focusing on the cross, instead of yourself or your ideas.

When you read each of these sections throughout the book, let my words lead you into the presence of God where you can hear His words to you personally. I have designed the Soul Soak with three sections.

The first section is "**The Blessing.**" As a reader of this book, God has placed you in my care for a little while; it is my privilege to minister to you as you read. I am honored to be your tour guide along this part of your journey with God. With this in mind, I want to extend a blessing to you each time you enter the Soul Soak. Blessings are a powerful force used by the Holy Spirit. If you remember, Jacob went to great lengths to steal Esau's blessing (see Genesis 25:30-34).

The second section of the Soul Soak is "**The Meditation.**" Here you will find several questions designed to help you enter into a time of intimacy with God. Prayerfully let the Holy Spirit probe your heart as you answer these questions.

The last section is "**The Prayer.**" Commit yourself to your new discoveries by completing the prayer I have begun for you in each Soul Soak. My prayer for you is that you discover peace and confidence in the sovereignty of God. The journey I have taken in bringing this book to completion has helped me to understand that each believer is on a personal journey. That journey has specific destinations coordinated by the Holy Spirit, according to our life choices. This journey will lead us to the ultimate goal of our Father, which is to make us a spotless bride for his Son, Jesus. Each true believer will reach this goal, not because we are deserving of the privilege and position of the bride of Christ, but because of the Father's immense love for his son, Jesus. Jesus deserves to have a spotless bride. The Father will settle for nothing less. God said it will happen, and so it will.

We must trust in the power of God to do what He says He will do. Not just in our own life, but in the life of every believer. I no longer feel like I have to fix people. I realize I am responsible to people but not for them. This truth has made ministry much easier for me. I know that God will go with people and help them end up where he wants them to be, even if they make all the wrong choices in getting there. May God bless you with the same trust in His sovereignty, for yourself and those you love.

"The journey is the destiny"

My college professor Ruth Breush used to say, "The journey is the destiny." Over the years, I have come to realize the power of her words. God does not have His eyes on the destination (where we are going and who we are going to be). Instead, God is much more interested in the relationship we develop with Him along the way.

It's like a man and a woman on vacation. Most men want to get where they are going. Women want to stop for lunch or go to the outlet mall they see along the way. For most men, vacation does not start until they arrive at the desired location. The woman, on the other hand, is on vacation the second she locks the door to her house behind her. God is not in a big hurry. He will often allow us to take side tracks along the way. If we want to stop at the "outlet mall" along the freeway of our destiny He lovingly goes with us. God will cause us to end up where He wants us to go. Of course we are much better off going the way God wants us to go, but if we do not, God does not abandon us. He causes all things to work together for our good (Romans 8:28). Understanding this principle has made ministry much easier for me. I can teach the way and let God help those who get side tracked.

It does not matter what you struggle with in your life today; God's love is irresistible. He will captivate your heart. Each stage of the journey we go through will prepare us to reign with the King and draw us into greater intimacy with our bridegroom.

There are no short cuts or detours with God. His plans for us are based upon His intimate knowledge of each of us. We need to just sit back and let the Holy Spirit direct us. When we learn to trust in the sovereignty of God, we gain the courage and confidence we need to surrender everything to Jesus. That is what this book is all about.

If you are desperate to know God's ways, if your heart cries out for greater understanding, if you have an unquenchable desire to know the Lord intimately and worship Him with all of your might, then this book is for you. If you are not as passionate for the Lord as you want to be, then keep reading. God has led you to this book.

He wants to set your heart aflame with the knowledge of His fervent love. No matter what, do not settle for what you know already. God is infinite and there is always more, always.

1
Disciple's Decision

Salvation saves you from hell, but discipleship saves you from yourself.

For God so loved the world that He gave His one and only son, that whoever believes in him shall not perish but have eternal life.

John 3:16

This scripture is adored by all who have made a commitment to Jesus Christ and memorized by Sunday school pupils the world over, but John 3:16 is also familiar to anyone who has ever watched a football game on TV. We live in a society where the Bible is one of many "holy books" and just about anyone who goes to church on Sunday, and even some who don't, considers himself a Christian.

No matter how watered down the contemporary version, the word *Christian* still means, "Little Christ." The character of Jesus and the intimate relationship He had with our heavenly Father is the focus for every true believer. As Christians, we are to follow Jesus Christ with our whole heart, which involves considerably more than a Sunday obligation and an occasional prayer in times of need or want.

The love of Jesus is all consuming. Once you have tasted it, you are ruined for the world. Our relationship with Jesus is a constant discovery which requires love, faith, and hope. The reward is secured, but the destiny is the journey. The Father is far more interested in our relationship with His Son than He is in getting us some place or making us someone. If we are going to travel this journey peacefully we must learn to see things as the Holy Spirit decides they are, not as we decide.

Often we lose our peace because we are afraid to find out what God wants. Instead of surrendering to our heavenly Father because He knows what is best for us, we try to bargain for our own way. Years ago, a good friend of mine gave birth to a very ill child who was not expected to live. Of course, the Christian community began to pray for a healing. However, the parents went to God for His plan instead of pursuing their own. God told them the child would be with Him in heaven. It amazed me to see the faith of these parents in surrendering their child to God. I was even more amazed to see the reaction of several of the Christians closest to the family. My friends were tormented in their grief by Christians who cursed them saying, "If this child dies it will be your fault for not having faith." Not having faith! These parents peacefully surrendered to the will of God while some of the Christians around them used their "faith" to try and manipulate God. If we are going to call ourselves Christians we must be like Christ who completely surrendered to the Father.

Convert or Disciple

The first step in the Christian journey is ***conversion***. This is the realization, brought on by the Holy Spirit, that we are sinners in need of a savior. We accept Jesus Christ into our lives and acknowledge his death and resurrection as the only payment for our sin.

The next step is that of ***discipleship***. Many Christians never progress to this step in their Christian walk. Without the power of God released into the life of a surrendered disciple, the church is left so weak that the world pays little attention to us.

There is a huge difference between a convert and a disciple of Christ. A convert believes Jesus Christ is the way to heaven, however, a convert still maintains the Lordship of his own life. Jesus is only one part of a convert's life. A true disciple, on the other hand, has completely abandoned his life to the Lordship of Jesus Christ. Their life is rooted in the Word of God and guided by the Holy Spirit. To a disciple, human reasoning and carnal desires must always surrender to the Holy Spirit's conviction.

The number one distinguishing factor between a convert and a disciple is the level of passion. Even though a disciple of Christ is not perfect, the passion of their heart is to serve Jesus Christ. This passion compels them to follow hard after the Savior no matter the cost.

A convert, however, has competing passions that are stronger than his or her passion for Christ. Therefore, a convert will justify and make excuses for carnal thoughts and actions rather than repent and be justified through Christ. Those who choose to be just a convert often choose self justification; remaining spiritual toddlers and never maturing in their knowledge of the Lord. Hebrews speaks to this kind of Christian.

> *...You have become dull of hearing. For though by this time you ought to be teachers, you need someone to teach you... you have come to need milk and not solid food. For everyone who partakes only of milk is unskilled in the word of righteousness, for he is a babe. But solid food belongs to those who are of full age, that is, those who by reason of use have their senses exercised to discern both good and evil.*
>
> *Hebrews 5:11-14* NKJV

Remember, salvation will save you from hell, but discipleship saves you from yourself.

The disciple on the other hand, desires to be convicted by the Holy Spirit of carnal thoughts and actions, leading them to repentance and allowing God to give them the mind and character of Christ.

It is very important that you take a moment right now and evaluate your position in Christ. Have you made the decision to be a disciple of Christ or are you merely a convert? If you have not taken the step to make Jesus Lord of your life then close this book, get down on your knees and repent for trying to have things your own way. Jesus is the lover of your soul. He is passionately pursuing you. He loves you and wants to have your whole heart. Do not make the mistake of thinking that you can resist the irresistible love of God. He will capture your heart at one time or another, why not make it today?

The Struggle

At every stage in our Christian walk we will encounter struggles and surprises. As a disciple, we are formulating our beliefs. We are in a constant state of change and growth. This can be exciting or unsettling, depending on our perspective. If we are religious it will be hard for the Holy Spirit to guide us into all truth (see John 16:13).

This is true for several reasons: First, religion is man's way of trying to reach God. Therefore, religious people make the mistake of thinking God thinks as they do. Secondly, religious people are concerned more about traditions than truth. In combination, these errors lead religious people to think all their man-made traditions are God-given truth thus leaving little room for change.

God will never be disillusioned with us because He never had any illusions in the first place.

Some scientists tell us that our brain does not have the capacity to know that the information it has stored could be wrong. This means our first reaction will be negative to information that is different from the information we have already learned. This is why humility is required to follow the Lord. We must be open to the Holy Spirit changing our theology. Our theology can change, but God will not. If this scares you, then you may be holding on to your principles too tightly.

When we assume we know the truth we can miss God. Our faith must be in God, not our knowledge of God. Our finite knowledge will always fall short of who the infinite God really is.

> *For if we are beside ourselves (mad as some say), it is for God and concerns Him; if we are in our right mind, it is for your benefit…*
> *II Corinthians 5:13* AMP

Paul is saying, what I already know I tell others with confidence, but I will never allow what I know to make me presumptuous before God. Be like Paul. As you read this book submit everything you know to God for further instruction. Whenever you read something that challenges your thinking or may even offend your beliefs, stop reading and go to God.

I do not want to just teach what I know. My desire is to see the life of Christ established in you. This will not happen by a transfer of information. The life of Christ can only be imparted when you hear God speak to you personally. If I can provoke you to go to God, then this book will be a success, even if you do not agree with everything I say.

If you get shocked by your sin you are thinking too highly of yourself.

As a disciple of Christ our struggle is to keep learning, to keep growing. A mentor of mine by the name of David Richards once told me, "The great paradox of the Christian life is that once you have found

God, you must keep seeking Him." This man was nearly eighty when he died, but he spoke of God with the wide-eyed wonder of a child.

The Surprise

As a young Christian I was made aware of the responsibility I carried as a child of God. I rarely heard sermons about the love of God; they were usually about God's expectations of me. I knew the scripture taught that it was not by my own power but by God's.

However, I still felt God was expecting me to change myself by praying enough, reading my Bible enough and going to church enough. The problem was, I couldn't do any of these things enough. I felt defeated; believing that God was disappointed in me. I was still trying to gain God's approval through works instead of through the blood of Jesus.

I have been crucified with Christ and I no longer live, but Christ lives in me. The life I live in the body, I live by faith in the Son of God, who loved me and gave himself for me.

Galatians 2:20 NKJV

One day while studying Galatians 2:20, the Lord asked me, "What power does a dead man have?"

I answered, "None."

He replied, "Then why do you think I expect you to do anything?"

If we are crucified with Christ then we have no power of our own. So, if we mingle the law or our own efforts with grace we will only fail.

Wherefore the law was our schoolmaster to bring us unto Christ, that we might be justified by faith.

Galatians 3:25 NKJV

Faith does not exist under the law. For the law insinuates that we can actually live up to the law, or there would be no standard. God says, Jesus, and only Jesus, satisfies the law (see Hebrews 9:11-15). Therefore, we must expect God to change us; we cannot try to change ourselves. God will never be disappointed or disillusioned with us, because He never had any illusions in the first place.

If we understand that God expects to change us then we will not allow guilt and shame to drive us away from God's presence. It is important that we fellowship with God in His presence without shame, for when we do, God is able to heal us of our wrong thinking and cleanse us from our sin.

For instance, I used to spend the first ten minutes or more of a worship service unable to worship because of my guilt. I would feel unworthy because I did not read my Bible enough or I sinned too much that week. By the time I got into the presence of God the worship service was over and I was blaming the Pastor for quenching the Holy Spirit by ending the worship too soon. Remember, if you get shocked by your sin you are thinking too highly of yourself. The root of guilt is not humility, but pride. Guilt infers that I have the ability to be something more than a sinner in need of a savior. No matter how long we have been saved we are still nothing without Jesus. The word teaches us that Jesus is our righteousness (see Philippians 3:8-9). God does not expect us to live His life; rather He wants to live through our life.

Let me share with you how the Holy Spirit taught me this truth. During a worship service I began to get the sensation that I was floating in a pool of water. I began to think about the law of gravity which makes it impossible for me to float unless I am in water. The reason being, the law of buoyancy overrides the law of gravity. It does not matter how long I am in the water, the minute I get out of the water I can no longer float. I never changed, nor did the laws of physics, what changed was my location.

Romans 8 speaks of the law of sin and death and the law of the spirit of life, these are God's spiritual laws. Jesus is our righteousness. He is like the water, as long as I am in Christ I am no longer under the law of sin and death illustrated by the law of gravity. It is sin that weighs us down. In Christ the law of the spirit of life, which is represented by the law of buoyancy, enables me to rise above sin like floating.

We are sinners who fall short of the glory of God (see Romans 3:23). If we walk in the Spirit and keep our mind set on Christ we can rise above our nature to sin. If I understand who I am, guilt has no place in my life. I am nothing. Jesus is everything. As a side note, God taught me this while my mind was wondering in worship. So, pay attention to your thoughts when they wonder, it just might be God speaking to you.

Let's have a

The Blessing

I declare all guilt and shame to be removed from our hearts in Jesus' name. We will surrender to the grace of God. We will walk in intimacy with the Father, Son, and Holy Spirit, because of the blood of Calvary. We will not focus on our lifestyle but on our relationship with God.

The Meditation

1. Do you live with guilt and shame? Have you understood that this comes from pride and not humility?

2. Am I willing to be known for who I am, instead of hiding or denying my weaknesses?

3. What adjustments do I need to make to walk in grace and humility?

The Prayer

Lord, cleanse me of all guilt and shame. I want to live free through Your grace. Help me to…

Do not confuse guilt with conviction. Guilt is a negative feeling initiated by Satan to produce unworthiness and shame. Satan wants to drive us away from God by leading us to believe God is disappointed with us.

For God has not given us the spirit of fear; but
of power and of love and of a sound mind.

II Timothy 1:7 KJV

The word "fear" in this passage means, a feeling of disapproval. God is not disappointed with us; He wants to empower us, whereas Satan tries to minimize God in our eyes. Guilt says God does not really have unconditional love; He loves just like we do, conditionally.

When we receive guilt we believe God is disappointed with us; we feel condemned. Condemnation leads to further sin. Oftentimes we receive these feelings from well-meaning, yet misinformed spiritual leaders who try to shame us into repentance. This is religion, not a relationship with Jesus Christ.

Conviction is a positive feeling initiated by the Holy Spirit to produce Godly remorse and freedom from shame through repentance. When the Holy Spirit points out our sin, it is not to shame us or accuse us. Remember that is Satan's job (see Revelation 12:10). Instead, it is the Holy Spirit's desire to protect us from the outcome of sin, which is death. He also wants to remove anything that will hinder our relationship with the Father.

The proper response to conviction is freedom through repentance and forgiveness of our sin. God's love overwhelms us and we lose the desire to sin. Conviction is simply the Holy Spirit saying that He is about to remove the sin because it is doing you harm (see I John 1:9). When God brings conviction into our life, it is just like a loving parent removing matches from the hands of a curious toddler. If that toddler could understand the danger he held in his hand he wouldn't feel bad about it being taken away. On the other hand, if he understood the danger he wouldn't be playing with it! This is the process of conviction and repentance.

What a relief to know that God is not disappointed with us and He does not expect us to live up to the expectations of the law. Instead God wants us to know His love and be empowered by His forgiveness. All we have to do is walk by faith. We must expect God to change us. This process begins by confessing our sin; not excusing it. Then we must ask God to show us why we desire the particular sin we have confessed. This allows the Holy Spirit to show us how to break our compulsion toward the sin.

For example, several years ago the Holy Spirit began to convict me about the types of TV programs I allowed myself to watch. I knew I needed to have more discretion, but I couldn't seem to resist. I prayed and asked God to remove my desire for the television.

One day I came down stairs to see my seven month old daughter sitting in her walker watching the television. The Holy Spirit gave me a vision of a demon coming out of the television and talking with my child. Now, I am very picky about what I watch. The Holy Spirit broke my compulsion for television not me. He changed my heart because he loves me and wants to protect me.

What a great love God has for us. God is not religious. He's not trying to shame us into righteousness. He is our redeemer. He does not expect us to make ourselves holy. He will make us holy when we yield ourselves without shame into His loving care. Do not be afraid to confess your sin before God. Ask Him to show you your own heart. He will reveal the truth that will set you free. Do not hide from God because of shame or guilt. Come out into the open with God, fall into His loving arms and allow Him to heal you.

The decision of the disciple is to keep growing, to keep allowing God to change him or her into the image of His son; to never allow what he already knows to keep him from knowing more.

It will come as a pleasant surprise to realize God will never be disillusioned with us, because he never had any illusions in the first place.

Notes

More Notes

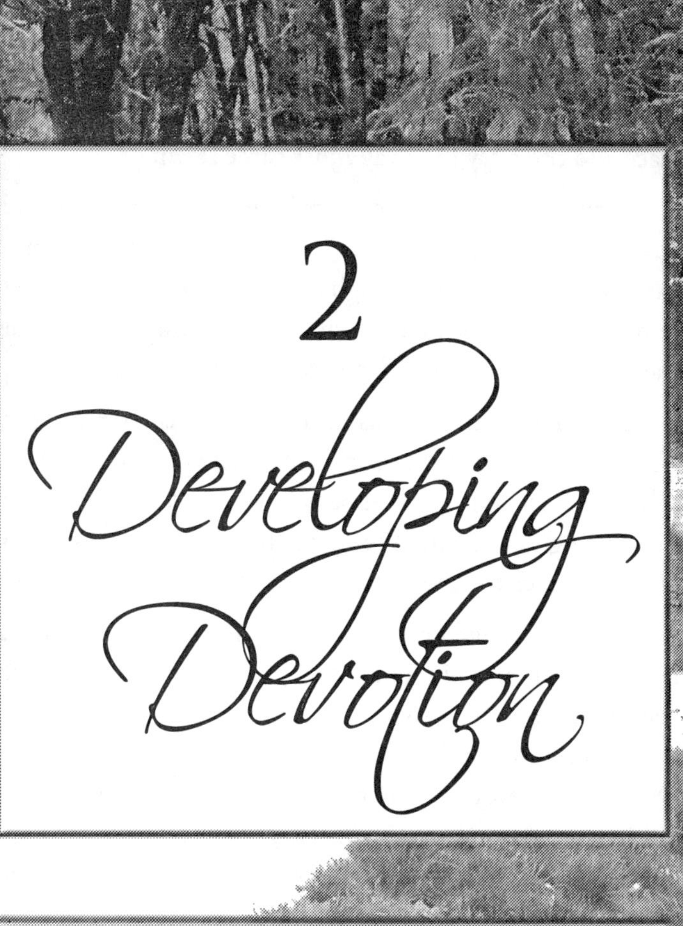

2 Developing Devotion

Having "devotions" is about obligation, having devotion is about passion.

One day I was driving down a busy street with construction crews on either side. In the midst of this chaos I heard the Lord direct me to pull off at a nearby park. I walked down along a stream that was shaded by beautiful oak trees. I sat down in the cool grass and let my feet touch the water's edge. What an instant contrast between this place and the busy highway I just came from.

In the background I could still hear the sounds of loud machinery and busy traffic. I could imagine the hectic hearts whizzing by in their cars that weren't going fast enough to keep up with their busy schedules. Just a minute before I was one of them, complaining to myself about how long it was going to take to finish the construction on that road.

Then my attention was drawn toward the stream that quietly moved along its path. I watched the water easily guided by a log or rock or some other obstacle in its path. The water never stopped; it was just redirected. Everything here seemed to move in harmony without business meetings or committees to rewrite the bylaws.

The Lord began to speak to me about the need to quiet my spirit so I, too, could be easily guided. I realized that day that the interruptions over which we often lose our peace are there for a reason. We easily miss the purpose of God in our lives because we are just too busy to notice. Developing devotion is not about having a set period of time we give to God everyday so we can be in charge of the rest of the day. No, developing devotion is about quieting our spirits so that God has control of our entire day.

Since you are my rock and my fortress, for the sake of your name lead and guide me. Free me from the trap that is set before me, for you are my refuge. Into your hands I commit my spirit, redeem me, oh Lord, the God of truth.

Psalm 31:3-5

The Struggle

When I was younger I spent a great deal of time in the local park near my home. My favorite spot in the park was the thirty foot waterfall. I would walk down the side of the embankment until I reached the foot of the falls. When the water level was low (usually in autumn) I could walk out on the large stones and sit right under the falls. I would sit there for hours and talk to Jesus. One day while sitting in my familiar spot, the Lord asked me why I came there all the time. After pondering it, I concluded I went there because the sound of the water was soothing and helped me block out the business of my life so I could pray.

The Lord spoke to me and said He wanted the Holy Spirit to be like the waterfall to me. He wanted His presence to sooth and quiet my spirit whenever I just thought about Him. At that moment, I felt God's presence more powerfully than I had ever felt it before. His presence became like the sound of the water within my spirit. Now I feel His presence whenever I just call on Him. Shortly after that day at the falls, the park closed the path to the bottom of the falls. God knew I would not be able to go there any more! God is an awesome God!

The voice of the Lord is over the waters.

Psalm 29:3

Mightier than the thunder of the great waters, the Lord on high is mighty

Psalm 93:4

Developing devotion is about quieting our spirits so that God has control of our entire day.

The time we spend alone in God's presence should never have to be a struggle. However, the process of developing devotion is often riddled with difficulty. Psalm 91:1 states:

> *He who dwells in the secret place of the most high shall remain stable and fixed under the shadow of the Almighty.* AMP

What exactly is the secret place of the most high? This is the ability to shut out the world and our carnal thinking to hear God's voice. This is what is meant by quieting our spirit or practicing God's presence.

When we first begin this process it may require a great deal of atmosphere just to keep us focused on God and not ourselves. For instance, we may need to put on quiet music and soften the lights. Some may feel like that would put them to sleep, so they go to a public place with a cup of coffee and a laptop. Whatever, the goal is to get to the place where props are no longer necessary to be in God's presence. We want to be able to hear God speak to us when we are shopping, in an elevator, at a football game or in the middle of an argument. The key is to practice His presence during our quiet times, so in the middle of our hectic lifestyles the small still voice of God can be recognized.

Read one verse and spend ten minutes pondering how that verse applies to your life.

As a Pastor I have spent a lot of time listening to the struggles of the Christian life. One complaint I hear often is "God never speaks to me". That simply is not true. The real problem is many of us do not recognize or even hear God's voice. It is much like television or radio waves, they are always in the air, but only those with the receptor on can hear what is playing. So, how do we turn on our God receptor?

How do we quiet our spirit? How do we practice God's presence? How do we develop devotion?

First, if we want to develop devotion we must expect God to speak to us!

It amazes me how many Christians read the Bible every day without giving the Holy Spirit the opportunity to speak to them. There is a big difference between reading, studying, and meditating on the Word. Many Christians set goals to achieve reading a certain number of chapters a day. Although it is commendable to read the Bible in its entirety, this may be more of a hindrance than a help if we want to hear God speak to us personally.

You see, while we are whizzing through our chapters for the day the Holy Spirit isn't able to get a word in edgewise. It is better to read one verse and spend ten minutes pondering how that verse applies to your life than to read all the chapters you require yourself to read that day.

If you're going to set a goal for yourself, make it a goal to receive something personal from your Bible reading every time you read. Do not be satisfied just learning what happened in the Bible, learn to ask the Holy Spirit questions. For example, "why does the book of Ephesians tell us not to be drunk with wine, but be filled with the Holy Spirit?" If you ask that kind of question and expect to get an answer you will. It will take time; do not give up too soon. Press on and expect God to speak to you. Be like Jacob, who refused

Read the Bible to discover God's character and to learn more about Him personally.

to give up until he got a blessing, so he wrestled with the angel all night. By the way, God told me being filled with the Spirit gives us the same relief from our problems as getting drunk, only instead of masking the problems, they get solved and you don't have a hangover in the morning. You see, if you ask questions and expect an answer, you will get one!

Secondly, if you are going to develop devotion, do not doubt when God does speak to you. All too often we hear God's voice, but as soon as things go bad we doubt ourselves. We question if we have heard God correctly. How can we be led by the Spirit if we are never willing to trust that we heard Him speak? Do not lose in the darkness what you receive in the light!

> If any of you lacks wisdom, he should ask God... But when he asks, he must believe and not doubt, because he who doubts is like a wave of the sea, blown and tossed by the wind. That man should not think he will receive anything from the Lord: he is a double-minded man, unstable in all he does. (James 1:5-8)

Cherish the desert experiences and don't be afraid, as though you are losing hold of God.

Thirdly, to develop devotion, read the Bible looking for the character of God; not solutions to your problems.

I remember asking God why I struggled reading the Bible. He said, "You're spending time with yourself and all your problems instead of with Me." At that time, I read to find out what sin I had or how to solve something. Now I read the Bible to discover God's character and to learn more about Him personally. It makes devotion time much more enjoyable to actually spend time with God instead of our problems. So, if you want to develop devotion, expect God to speak to you. Do not doubt when He does. Ask the Holy Spirit questions about the Word, and read the Bible to discover more about God personally. If you do these things on a regular basis, you will develop devotion for Jesus.

The Surprise

I have been a Christian most of my life. By the time I was fifteen I was preaching the gospel on a regular basis. At eighteen years of age I answered the call to full time ministry. At twenty eight I had already preached the gospel in six different nations of the world. At twenty nine the Lord saw fit to bring a husband into my life. After being in the ministry for nearly ten years as a single person, this was like slowing down a runaway train.

I can remember telling my husband I felt like I was losing my passion for the Lord. Instead of being consumed with the work of God all I wanted to do was be with my new husband.

My husband wisely said, "Honey, you're not losing your passion, your just becoming passionate about different things." Have you ever been in a place like this? It seems like the passion that you once had for a specific something is gone. Maybe circumstances have changed your schedule, or even your perspective, and your connection to the Lord feels like it is slipping.

I have always heard these times referred to as dry periods in our Christian walk. Well-meaning but misinformed friends would tell me I just needed to be more disciplined, but that only added guilt to my disappointment. I remember thinking, if I am in love with God, why is spending time with Him a discipline, shouldn't I want to be with Him?

I do not have to discipline myself to spend time with my husband; I want to be with him. The Holy Spirit led me to the truth about these dry times. They are like the farmer who tends his fields. If the farmer keeps his fields too watered, they will not grow deep roots. Instead, he waters his plants periodically, leaving times of dryness in between so the roots grow deep in search of water.

God comes to us in similar cycles, refreshing us in times of closeness and strengthening us in times of dryness.

Then Jesus was lead by the Spirit into the desert...
Matthew 4:1

Once I realized that these dry times were not a punishment for wrong doing or an indication that I was some how backsliding, I was able to relax and trust God to bring me through them. I also realized that just like the trees in winter, growth takes place in the times of barrenness.

Fruitfulness is the celebration of that growth. In reality, we are actually growing spiritually when we seem disconnected from God. He refreshes our spirit in seasons of closeness by revealing to us what happened in the desert. So, we aren't growing when we feel spiritual. We are actually celebrating the growth of the dry season.

It is a nice surprise to realize that God has ordained dry seasons in our lives. When we realize this, guilt can no longer rob us of the purpose for these times. We must learn to cherish the desert experiences and not be afraid, as though somehow we are losing hold of God. No, God holds on to us.

The Father Himself is the initiator; He will draw us by His spirit to pray, read the Word and worship if we will stop trying to discipline ourselves. When we trust the Lord to lead us, we discover that God is the one sustaining us; not our devotional life.

If the Lord delights in a man's way, He makes his steps firm; though he stumble, he will not fall, for the Lord upholds him with His hand.
Psalm 37:23

The struggle in developing devotion is quieting our spirit; the ability to shut the world out and hear God's voice (See Psalm 91:1).

The surprise is that God initiates our devotion. We do not have to discipline ourselves to have devotion time; we have to allow God to draw us.

Notes

Notes

3

Growing in Grace

We cannot have grace for others
until we have it for ourselves.

I was raised in a strong Christian home. My parents had a good marriage and exercised loving discipline in our lives. I am the oldest of four children and all of us have served the Lord from an early age. My father went into the ministry in his early forties when I was already in high school. This transition wasn't that difficult. The only difference was he was finally getting paid to serve in ministry, plus he only had to work one job. My father was a pastor long before he realized it. I tell you all this because it played an important role in my understanding of grace.

You see, I preached about grace long before I was able to live by it. I guess I only understood grace for the "sinner" and after all, with my upbringing, I really didn't need grace, or so I thought. I thought that all my "good works" were impressing God, until one day God said to me, "Joy, I can never be impressed by what you do for Me, because I either did it Myself through you or you did things yourself from a heart of rebellion." Did you know you can do good works with wrong motives?

From God's perspective, anything done with an impure motive is rebellion. It doesn't matter how religious or successful the work is (see I Corinthians 3:10-23). Let me give you an example. The year I got married, God decided to bless me with everything I wanted all at once. In one year, I was married, bought my first house, was ordained as a minister, and had my first child. Wow! What a year! However, something was looming over my head, I felt extremely guilty for being so blessed. What made it worse was that a fellow pastor was dying of cancer at a young age during this same year. Why was I so blessed and he was not?

I then decided the "Christian" thing to do would be to sacrifice the new chandelier I wanted for my new dinning room and bless my friends instead. I was feeling pretty good about this plan until God revealed my heart to me. I was trying to bribe God! The Lord showed me that I was afraid I had too much blessing, so I better even out the score a little bit before God did. Wow! I was trying to manipulate the Lord with my "good deed." This also revealed a major misconception I had about the character of God that we will discuss later in this chapter. It is very important that we are sensitive to the Holy Spirit's probing when it comes down to our motives. It will be much easier to face the truth now about our deceitful hearts than to stand shocked and amazed as we watch our works of wood, hay, and stubble burn up before the Lord (see I Corinthians 3:12). The reality is many of us do not understand God's grace; if we did we would not judge ourselves or others according to worldly measures of success.

I believe more of us than not will be shocked by the standards in which God judges our works. It will be too late by then to realize that God isn't impressed by the same things we are! Take missions money for instance; I wonder how much of it was raised by wrong motives! Many Christians are manipulated and even coerced into giving their money. Ouch! Won't we be shocked that while people might be singing, "Thank you for giving to the Lord," the Lord Himself might just have His head hung down with disappointment.

God will never be impressed by our works, because he either did them Himself or we did them from a heart of rebellion.

In I Corinthians, Paul is talking about our works being judged, but in verse 9 he indicates that we are the building being built. So our works should be building our hearts, not the kingdom. Remember, God is the one who builds the Kingdom not us (see Psalm 127:1). Our works should demonstrate our godly character, not our talents or gifts. God will not be impressed if we gain success in the kingdom through ungodly virtues. This perspective will change how we do things for God, and when it does, the church will truly rise in God's power as she should.

The Struggle

So, why is grace so hard for us to understand? Basically, because our pride hates it. To live by grace is to admit that we are nothing and can do nothing unless God does it. Now we know that in theory, but do we really live it?

> ***Religion works from the outside in, the emphasis is on lifestyle. Grace works from the inside out, the emphasis is on relationship.***

...Continue to work out your salvation in fear and trembling, for it is God who works in to will and to act according to His good purpose.

Philippians 2:12-13

Religious folks love this passage because they think it holds us responsible to live for the Lord. We have to work out our own salvation, right? Can you see the subtle influence of pride in this interpretation? Pride wants the emphasis placed on us. If we get the responsibility we also get the praise or blame and can make ourselves feel good and others bad. What Paul is saying in this passage is that God is the one who puts in you the desire to do good and then the ability to do it.

So, all we have to do is work out what God put in us. This is grace. This is God getting the glory not man! The emphasis is on God.

For many years I only understood grace for the "sinner" or the new convert. Unfortunately, even the new convert had only a small window of time before he too had a standard by which to live. Religion works from the outside in, the emphasis is placed on lifestyle. Grace, however, works from the inside out, the emphasis is on the relationship.

Suppose a young woman spots an attractive man from across a crowded room. They make eye contact and then exchange smiles, soon the man is approaching. What does she say? What will he say? Her heart is pounding with anticipation; could he be the one? As he approaches he opens with a warm gesture and then a heart melting compliment.

Just about the time her heart gives into this moment of eternal passion... wait what did he say? He wants her to wash his clothes for him and cook him dinner every night? Who does he think he is? That's it. It's over. She didn't really like his hair. Oh, and his shirt was ugly and how about the way he walks? She politely excuses herself and with a roll of her eyeballs, turns on her heel and is out of there.

Believe it or not, this is a picture of what religion does to people. God is somewhat attractive to us from a distance. But then, before we know it, we establish all these expectations God wants us to meet. No wonder so many people have no interest in God these days.

Now, let us suppose that same young couple started to get to know each other. They spent time together laughing and enjoying each other's company. Soon that list of expectations would become the things she wants to do for this man she loves. The relationship turned the list of responsibilities into the desires of a woman in love. This is what the grace of God is all about. It does not excuse sin as some argue; rather it empowers the believer to live for God.

I remember when I first got into the ministry I felt called to the streets. I know now I loved street ministry because grace worked there. I had no expectations for the prostitute or the crack addict. I knew all I had to do was to love them. God was the one who did the work.

On the other hand, I hated church ministry because my expectations for Christians were extremely high. I felt God was holding me responsible to fix the wrong, because I was a pastor. Paul says:

Are you so foolish? After beginning with the Spirit, are you now trying to attain your goals by human effort?

Galatians 3:3

When God started to deal with me about my lack of grace toward the church, He showed me I would never have grace for others until I had it for myself. I had never been able to live up to the expectations I had placed on others either, but at least I felt very guilty about it. I saw others failing but they did not seem to carry any guilt about it.

This lack of concern is what fueled my anger and criticism. God was so merciful to show me that my real frustration was toward myself. I wanted so badly to be just like Jesus, but I was failing miserably. I was passionate and faithful to God but my weaknesses were many. How could I be pleasing to the Lord? There was so much at stake in my life that I was defensive toward anyone who tried to show me where I was wrong.

I was so confused that I even mistook the voice of God for my flesh. I was getting ready to graduate Bible College about this time and had found a place of ministry in Orlando, Florida. I heard a voice deep inside telling me to go home instead, but I dismissed that as my flesh. As a Bible college graduate, I felt it was my obligation to be in the ministry. So, I went to Orlando for nine miserable months, until one night the Lord told me, "You will go home immediately!"

I was convinced that I was dying of cancer or something, because in my mind, that was the only reason God would send me home. After all, I was willing to suffer in the ministry, surely God would take advantage of that if He could. As I lay on my bed trying to accept this martyrdom God was asking of me, an amazing thing happened.

I started to remember the feeling I would get when I would hear the garage door go up as a young girl. This meant Dad was home from something very important that he had been doing. Remember, I told you at the beginning of this chapter the kind of dedicated man my father was. I was not to be just hanging around doing nothing. I had to get busy. So, I would jump off the couch and get busy. It didn't matter what, I just had to be doing something.

While I was remembering this experience from childhood the Lord gently said, "I am not your earthly father and you do not have to be doing something to make Me happy. I want you to go home and rest. College has been stressful and I want you to rest for a little while".

Oh, the tears flowed that day and God began a tremendous work of grace in my heart. Our heavenly Father is so incredibly loving, kind, and gentle. When we discover the true nature of God it leads us to repentance (Romans 2:4).

The mere thought of God's affirmation is energizing. Now that is the power of grace!

The Surprise

Once I got home from college the real work of the Spirit began in my heart. It was very painful, but I am so very thankful for it now. One thing about the devil, he will always tell you what it will cost you to obey God, but he never tells you what it will cost you to disobey. Of course, the cost is always greater to disobey God.

There were many times that I questioned God during that time right after college. I felt as if He told me to go home and be a nominal Christian. The only thing I was allowed to do was go to church on Sunday. This was extremely painful since I had always preached a message of works. Now I had to come home to these same people and do nothing. That was very humiliating to me, not to mention confusing.

One day I was at the waterfall I mentioned in the last chapter (this was before the experience I told you about) and I was very upset. I was crying out to God asking what is going on. Why did you call me to the ministry, send me off to Bible College and tell me to do nothing? As I was praying I began to have a vision (a picture in your mind's eye that comes from God).

I saw myself sitting on the rocks by the falls crying. Then I saw that same picture inside a big black caldron. There was a hand inside the pot spinning me around and around. I knew that the hand was the hand of God. So, I began arguing with Him, "You are not the God of confusion, why are you doing this to me"? Next, the vision opened again and I saw the whole image of God standing outside the caldron I was in. It was a huge reflection of me. The Lord spoke to me and said, "You love Me with all your heart and you are serving Me faithfully, but this is your concept of who I am. I have brought you home to reveal to you who I really am." After that day I began a journey toward an intimate relationship, rather than a working relationship with Jesus. It has been sixteen years since that day and I am still growing in grace.

Shortly after that day at the waterfall I was sitting with a pastor friend just talking about the Lord. She asked me what I thought to be a very peculiar question at the time. She asked, "Have you ever just sat and let God affirm you?"

"Affirm me? You have got to be kidding. For what?"

"Just because He loves you", was her reply.

Wow! I had never even considered that God could be proud of me, after all the times I failed Him. The mere thought of it energized me in a way I had never known before. God wants to affirm me! Wow! Oh, the power of God's grace! It makes me sad to think of all the Christians that are trapped like I was. It also saddens me to think about all the pastors that carry this tremendous load of responsibility and how they are just dumping it on their congregations. But the day is coming and will soon be, when God will lavish His favor upon the church.

It will not come because we have prayed enough or worshipped enough or purified our lives enough. No, the day of God's favor is coming simply because He is a good God.

The greatest surprise I received from the Lord during this journey of grace was the day he freed me from my pastoral obligations. No, he did not fire me! I was in a worship service sitting on the platform

Satan will always tell you what it will cost you to obey God. He will never tell you what it costs to disobey.

just enjoying the Father's presence when all of a sudden He spoke to me. He said, "Joy, I do not hold you any more responsible than anyone else in the room."

When He said that, I could feel this tremendous weight just lift right off of me. I realized that I believed God was counting on me to be the hero. I thought He was holding me personally responsible for everything I knew the church could be. I imagined God saying to me, "Come on Joy, you have to do it, everyone else has let me down."

This is referred to as the Elijah Syndrome. Remember, Elijah thought he was the only one who had not bowed his knees to the false God, Baal (I Kings 19:10). If you have a prophetic gifting, be very cautious of this mentality.

God does not want you to carry this burden. In fact, I believe the double portion anointing that Elisha received was to have grace added to the prophetic gift. God's grace makes the burden of prophetic ministry much easier to bear. As a result, prophetic people with the double portion anointing are more gracious to others.

What a nice surprise to realize that God wants to affirm you and that He's not holding you personally responsible for the work of God. Let God release you from the burden of obligation. His yoke is easy and His burden is light (Matthew 11:30). If the Holy Spirit is ministering to you right now, then close the book and let Him speak to you. Maybe you have misconceptions that burden you that are different from the ones I have mentioned. Jesus wants to set you free, so practice quieting your spirit right now, so he can speak.

The struggle to grow in grace is about letting go of pride and religious thinking.

Notes

More Notes

4

Pursuing Passion

Passion is holiness, not enthusiasm, and holiness is attitude not action.

"O God, you are my God, earnestly I seek you; my soul thirsts for you, my body longs for you, in a dry and weary land where there is no water. Because your love is better than life, my lips will glorify you."

Psalm 63:1,3

If I were to sum the whole of scripture up into one word, that word would be passion. Passion is like a purple velvet ribbon cascading over and through every page, it floats and winds and curves through every heart that penned each line of God's Holy Word.

Passion is the common declaration that threads together the years, experiences and individuals that embody scripture. Its echo has been heard down through the centuries as it was first voiced by God Himself in the garden, when He said, "it is good."

Passion is the very heart of God. It is expressed through the wisdom of the Father in crafting the plan of salvation, it is demonstrated through the sacrifice of Jesus in fulfilling the Father's plan, and it is imparted, through the guidance of the Holy Spirit in communicating the Father's plan to us, the children of God.

Passion for God is the one thing the devil hates the most, because it is the one thing that moves the heart of God the most (see James 5:16). He goes to great lengths to quench it, prevent it, and distort it. Satan has a plan to steal from God the joy He receives when our hearts are passionate for Him. I do not believe the enemy really thinks he will beat God. He is far too smart and has seen too much to be that naive.

Quite simply, his jealousy and hatred have consumed him to the point that losing isn't the problem. Satan just doesn't want God to win our hearts. If Satan can take us down with him he will have accomplished his goal. So you see, with that in mind, it isn't good enough for me that Satan will be defeated in the end. I do not want to see God lose one passionate heart. We are at war, and it will be costly, even deadly, but that will not stop the passionate ones.

Fear is having an agenda different than God's. When I have surrendered my heart and have been consumed by the passion of God, no price is too high, for God's Glory is the prize. We cannot waste time being carnal. This life is but a vapor (James 4:14). Christian, what are you spending your time doing? Are your goals temporal, will they only mean something in this lifetime? When your short life is over, will the success you achieved mean anything in eternity? Are you holding on to things that will fade and letting go of the eternal?

> *We do, however, speak a message of wisdom among the mature, but not the wisdom of this age or the rulers of this age, who are coming to nothing. No, we speak of God's secret wisdom, a wisdom that has been hidden and that God destined for our glory before time began.*
>
> *I Corinthians 2:6-7*

What does it mean to be passionate for the Lord? When we are captivated by the love, wisdom, gentleness, and kindness of God, when we are convinced that the inferior pleasures of sin cannot be compared to the joy of intimate relationship with God, then we are passionate. "Passionate" is not a word to be given to someone with enthusiasm or a perky personality. Passion is about holiness, character, and love. I can dance in the presence of the Lord, but if my heart is not broken by my sin I am not

Fear is having an agenda different than God's.

passionate for God. I can quote scripture and display great spiritual gifts, but if I have no grace for those of weaker faith I am not passionate for God.

Pursuing passion is about pursuing an intimate relationship with Jesus Christ, one that causes us to want the same things that Jesus wants, hate what He hates and do what He does. Religion can manipulate us through fear to accept what Jesus wants, feel guilt about what he hates and do what He does when others are watching.

This falls so short of what God desires for us. He wants to reveal himself to us and to impart who He is in us. What a difference there is between a passionate relationship with Jesus and just having a religious lifestyle.

{Evildoers} wander about for food and howl if not satisfied. But I will sing of your strength, in the morning I will sing of your love; for you are my fortress, my refuge in times of trouble.

Psalm 59:15-16

If we want to stop sinning we must destroy the lie that keeps drawing us back to the sin.

This scripture pictures a completely satisfied heart in God. The psalmist has tasted the superior pleasures of God and no longer looks to be satisfied by other things. My prayer is that every believer will come to this realization.

It is safe to trust in the Lord. We do not have to make excuses any longer for not obeying God. We are content to follow Him wherever He leads, we have no fear. It will happen. God will bring His

Church to this place of rest. The bride of Christ will be spotless when she meets her bridegroom face to face.

The Struggle

I believe that most Christians have good intentions; they want to serve the Lord. Yet if this is so, why is the church so weak? Why do we not see the power of God in our lives like the scripture describes? Why is victory a goal just beyond our reach when the Word says that every believer walks in victory? It is because our statements of belief are not as real as our true inner feelings. Many of us are desperately trying to cling to what we know is true, yet experience has taught us differently. Like the Christian woman who knows God loves her, yet wonders why He wasn't there to stop her father from molesting her as a child.

We have statements of belief that we really want to believe, but if we are honest, we do not. We have been told that if we quote the scripture to ourselves enough the bad feelings will go away. Or even worse, some have been told they lack faith because they do not come to church enough, or pray enough, or some other shortcoming is the reason. All of this is religious talk.

If you have received this kind of advice ask God to set you free from it. How can you be passionate toward a God you do not trust to help you? We are told to cast our cares on Jesus, but how do we do that? How does the father who cannot find work tithe? Why does a loving God command me to give to Him what I need to feed my family?

Is the church adequately answering these questions or are we adding insult to injury by saying, "You just have to believe, brother!" These responses to real questions are an indication that we really do not know

God's heart. Many of us just do what we are told and expect others to do the same. We do not take the time to discover the heart of God and why He requires certain things of us. We do not take the time to help people heal from past hurt, we just tell them, "It's all under the blood," meaning that the death of Jesus has taken care of everything. Well, it is all under the blood, but how do I leave it there?

Holiness is the process of becoming separated from the world and set apart unto God. This is not about actions; it is about attitudes (remember I can do the right things for the wrong reasons). We all have attitudes or perspectives that are not in line with the Word of God. We must allow the Holy Spirit to remove these things from us. What we need to be separated from is not sin, for that is already taken care of. We need separated from the lies our experiences have taught us. It is the lies the enemy put in our hearts over time that we must discover and let God destroy. These lies are what the Bible refers to as strongholds.

When we doubt God loves us, then we doubt that He wants to use us and we stop serving Him.

The weapons we fight with are not weapons of this world. They have divine power to demolish strongholds. We demolish arguments and every pretension that sets itself up against the knowledge of God, and we take captive every thought to make it obedient to Christ.

II Corinthians 10:4-5

This scripture is giving us the process of holiness. Our sin has been taken care of through the shed blood of Jesus Christ. Our sins are forgiven every time we ask, but if we want to stop sinning we must destroy the lie that keeps drawing us back to the sin.

How do we destroy the stronghold that keeps us from an intimate relationship with the Lord?

1. We need to ask the Holy Spirit to reveal the lies.
2. Wait until the Lord shows you something, like an event in your life or a person that hurt you.
3. Ask the Holy Spirit what lie you received from the memory.
4. Ask Jesus to tell you the truth.

Once the Holy Spirit is able to separate us from the lie then he can set us apart unto God. The Holy Spirit can then show you the reason you struggle with certain issues or people. We must learn to let the Holy Spirit be our "Comforter" (John 14:16). Once we learn that the Holy Spirit is not like our parents or our Pastors, who sometimes say, "...because I told you so," then we will trust Him to cleanse us from our sin.

For many years I struggled with guilt whenever someone was mad at me. I really had a hard time letting go of the guilt even after I reconciled the relationship. I knew the scriptures said I was forgiven, but I did not feel like I was. So, I asked the Lord to show me the lie that I really believed, instead of His Word that I wanted to believe.

He reminded me of my childhood friend Stephanie that I played jacks with on the playground after school. Her house was right next door to the school. Her brother would stand on the porch and say very mean things to me, I never knew why. I was so afraid of this boy that I would cross the street to go home instead of walk in front of his house.

While I was remembering this, the Lord said "You're not responsible for that boy's anger." Then the Lord impressed upon me that violence occurred inside that house. The little boy was jealous that his sister had an escape while he had to stay home. The Lord showed me that I still carried guilt over that boy being angry with me, so every time I was in a similar situation the guilt would come back. I realize now that I am not responsible for everyone's pain, like my experience taught me. God set me free from the guilt and now I can receive His forgiveness.

If you're struggling with believing God's Word even though you really want to and try to, just go to the Holy Spirit. He will comfort you and show you why you struggle in that situation, sin or feeling. God does not want you to carry this burden any longer. If you have never had God help you this way it may take a while for you to learn how to receive from Him, but do not give up. Pray this pray with me:

Father, I need you to reveal the truth to me. I do not want to live by the enemy's lies any longer. Please show me when I was lied to and cleanse me from the hurt. I want your Word to be real to me, not just something I try to believe but cannot. I thank you that you love me and you want to help me. Amen.

Remember, we have already learned that we must expect God to speak to us, so be looking for the answer. It just might come to you when you least expect it.

The Surprise

It does not take all the bells and whistles we think it does to get God's attention. The Lord wants to answer our prayers more than we want them answered. He really is for us.

The most surprising thing about pursuing passion for God, however, is that God really is the pursuer. He is passionately trying to get our attention. The story of Song of Solomon is the clearest picture we have of just how passionate God really is for us.

My dove in the cleft of the rock, in the hiding places on the mountainside, show me your face, let me hear your voice; for your voice is sweet, and your face is lovely. Catch for us the foxes, the little foxes that ruin the vineyards, our vineyards that are in bloom.

Song of Solomon 2:14-15

The beloved, who is the woman, is being chased by The Lover. He calls out to her not to hide from him. Her reply is to ask him to take away the things that can hinder their relationship. We often hide from the Lord because we feel like failures; we think that He is ashamed of us. But His heart is overwhelmed with love for us. Unfortunately, religion has portrayed a far different view of God's attitude toward us. Religion often leaves us believing that God is disappointed with us. When we believe that God is disappointed, it becomes hard to receive His grace and love. When we doubt God loves us, then we doubt that He wants to use us and we stop serving Him.

We must embrace God's forgiveness before we will embrace God's plan for our lives.

One night my husband and I were sitting together and I was telling him about a difficult situation I was having with someone at the church. I felt like I had failed as a pastor. The whole time I was talking to him he was smiling so lovingly, just gazing into my eyes and caressing my hair. I could tell his heart was saying "I love you for caring so much about this person." My heart was pierced through with God's passion for me as I gazed into my husband's soul that night.

Jesus is just like that for us. He calls to us when we are hiding from shame. He loves us so passionately; He truly is the lover of our soul. We do not have to cringe at the thought of all our failures. God loves us unconditionally.

One day a woman from my church approached me before the Sunday morning service. She began to tell me a story about her five year old daughter that had occurred over the previous week. She had been scolding her daughter for misbehaving and said to her "I am very disappointed with you and so is God."

Her daughter's reply was, "I serve a mighty God, Mom. He loves me no matter what. It is Satan who wants you to believe that God is mad at me!"

Wow! The woman asked me how she should have handled that. I said, "There is nothing you could have said, your five year old daughter was right!"

I shared that testimony in the church service that morning and God set many people free from guilt and shame!

It is because of God's great passion toward us that He designed the plan of salvation. When we understand God's heart for us we want to repent. We will live holy lives before Him when the passion of God consumes us. We must embrace God's forgiveness before we will embrace God's plan for our lives. It comes as a nice surprise to realize that God is the One pursuing us.

The struggle in pursuing passion is allowing Jesus to remove the lies that **keep us from receiving His passion for us.**

The surprise is that God is the one pursuing us. It is His passion that fills us when we stop hiding and embrace His forgiveness.

Let's have a

The Blessing

I release the fire of the Holy Spirit to consume all that is impure and less satisfying than the Father's love. I impart through the Holy Spirit a fresh passion for Jesus that will light our way and renew our minds. May all religious thinking that keeps us from embracing God's unconditional love be removed from our minds. Instead, may we receive a resolve and strength to live for Jesus through His grace.

The Meditation

1. Rate your passion for the Lord, then explain your answer.

Living below mediocrity | *Maintenance mode* | *Pursuing God* | *Desperate for His presence*

2. What religious thinking is preventing you from embracing God's unconditional love more passionately? What must you do to get rid of it?

The Prayer

Lord, I want to pursue you passionately. I do not want to just get by. I want my spirit to soar with You to new levels of revelation and anointing. Help me to...

Notes

More Notes

5

Desperate to Die

Life is the first central theme of the Bible. Death is the second.

"For to me, to live is Christ and to die is gain."

Philippians 1:21

The apostle Paul was desperate to die. He had such a passion for Christ and a reality of His glory that life on earth was merely tolerated for the sake of spreading the gospel. The love of God compelled Paul because he wanted others to experience the great love affair he had with Jesus (II Corinthians 5:14). Paul was not satisfied with Jesus having a part of his life; Jesus was his life. The impact of God's love caused him to sing God's praises, even though his obedience landed him in a dark damp prison cell. He transcended human need, fear and desire, which captivate and control most of us. I feel really good about my relationship with Christ if His love can compel me to stay calm in a traffic jam!

So, what is the secret to having the kind of joy that Paul had? Why, unlike Paul, is heaven only a distant dream for so many Christians instead of a reality that governs the life we live on earth? Why do we sing "I'll fly Away" in church, but have our hearts sink in fear when the doctor calls with our test results?

The Struggle

But a natural man does not accept the things of the Spirit of God; for they are foolishness to him, and he cannot understand them, because they are spiritually appraised.

I Corinthians 2: 14 NASB

Religion is man's way of trying to reach God. Humanity has a need created by God to be a part of something bigger than themselves. We fight to be in control because of pride, but we long for the safety of knowing we are being taken care of.

This struggle has birthed the "religious" system that many find temporary comfort in, yet it lacks relevance to the true Creator. For instance, we are inundated with religious jargon on television that focuses on the nobility of human faith, not God. People say things like, "My strong faith gets me through tough times."

No, it is not faith that gets us through, it is God. Humanism is the religion of choice these days. Man is in charge of his own destiny with a little help from the God of his own choosing. This kind of "faith" just demonstrates how out of touch we are with the truth. If there is a God (and of course there is), we must be accountable to Him. God is not accountable to mankind.

In search of the truth, we have diluted it. We shroud our arrogance with "tolerance" by centering our attention on the accommodation of human opinion. In the end, we have reduced the name of God to a motivational catch phrase. When are we going to realize that the natural man will never discern the spiritual? Human reasoning will never discover God's truth.

Truth is the man Jesus Christ (see John 14:6); He is known through divine revelation.

How then do we receive divine revelation?

"Whoever finds his life will lose it, and whoever loses his life for my sake will find it."

Matthew 10:39

We find temporary comfort in a religious system, yet it lacks relativity to the true Creator.

"Therefore, whoever humbles himself like this child is the greatest in the kingdom of heaven."
Matthew 18:4

If we really want to know the truth, then we must humble ourselves. We must give up our rights to control our own destiny and let God show us the way. I'm not just talking about the way to heaven. I'm talking about the way to pay our taxes, the way to raise our children, the way to treat our spouses. God needs to be calling the shots, and not just when His ways agree with ours. God's truth is not dependent upon our understanding. When we do not agree we must surrender our position to God in order for Him to reveal His way to us.

God wants us to understand Him, not just obey Him. Many Christians just do what they are told. They do not go to God in humility seeking understanding. When we obey without understanding or rebel without acknowledging God, intimacy with God is lost.

When we obey without understanding... intimacy with God is lost.

We have been created for intimacy. God invites us to draw near to Him (Isaiah 55:6). He wants us to be honest with Him instead of hiding or justifying ourselves. For instance, if we do not want to tithe (giving 10% of our income to the church) we must not make excuses as to why we cannot do it. We must not blame the pastor and tell ourselves he is just after our money.

If we want divine revelation we must humble ourselves, turn to the scriptures to guide us to the truth and ask God to show us why He asks us to tithe. On the other hand, do not tithe just because the church says to do so. You need to have an understanding. The scripture tells us to be ready in season and out to give an account to every man (see II Timothy 4:2).

Do not rebel and do not just obey, but seek God for His understanding. We must seek God's face, not just His hand. In other words, we must desire His friendship, not just His power. If we are seeking His face, we will ask Him what is His will in our situation. If we are seeking His hand or His power, we will beg Him to do things our way. By humbling ourselves we will be able to discern spiritual things. We will know God. If we give up [control of] our life then we will find it. Jesus is life!

The Blessing

You will walk humbly with your God. You will seek His face and not His hand. You will grow in revelation and spiritual knowledge. Your faith will be child-like and your desperation for God fierce.

The Meditation

1. How do you handle biblical truths that do not make sense to you logically?

- ❑ I ignore it and get defensive when the subject it brought up.
- ❑ I search the scriptures and pray until I gain the understanding I need to obey.
- ❑ I just obey God but it does not create resentment because I trust Him
- ❑ I obey God but deep down I feel afraid or resentful.
- ❑ Other ________________

2. How does it make you feel to hear that God wants to be intimate with you?
   - ❑ I am comfortable with my relationship with God as it is. I do not need it to change.
   - ❑ The word "intimate" is a little uncomfortable for me to associate with God. He is God, I do not think of Him in those familiar terms.
   - ❑ I was attracted to this book because I desire intimacy but I do not understand it.
   - ❑ I am desperate for more of God. I want to know the truth, even if it means discovering that I have been wrong about some things.

3. In what area of your life do you need to seek God's face instead of His hand?

____

____

____

The Prayer

Lord, forgive me for holding on to my own ideas about You and Your ways. I really do want to know You more intimately than I do today. Help me not to fear the unknown. I want to walk humbly with You so...

The Surprise

It is amazing what you will discover once you learn the secret of humility. One night during midweek prayer service God revealed my own heart to me. While I was praying, I began to visualize in my mind the most horrible, smelly, dung heap with maggots crawling all over it. God spoke to me and told me this was a picture of how my spiritual pride looked to Him. I began to weep and cry out in terror. For the first time I was truly understanding my own sinfulness.

Many of you experienced this kind of revelation when you were saved. For me however, being saved at an early age, the Spirit of God kept me from my true self. When I realized what I was truly like apart from God, I was horrified. After God assured me that I was still saved—I truly was questioning it—I began to thank Him that I was no longer like that dung heap.

Immediately, the Holy Spirit stopped me. He said, "Joy, the only reason why you're not crawling right back into that mess is because I have given you the desire to not go back there. I could remove My desire for holiness within you and you would crawl in that dung just like the maggots." You see, everything good in us comes from God, even our desire for good.

"For it is God who works in you to will and to act according to His good purpose."

Philippians 2:13

When we humble ourselves before God He shows us the truth so that we can understand it. We begin to take on the mind of Christ (Philippians 2:5-8). This process of humility, surrender and revelation is what Jesus is talking about in Matthew 16:24. Jesus tells us that we must deny ourselves in order to follow Him. Jesus' words stand in stark opposition to this day in age of self realization and empowerment.

What does it mean to "deny self?"

"Do not conform any longer to the patterns of this world,
but be transformed by the renewing of your mind."

Romans 12:2

This process of mind renewal works much the same way as when you go roller skating. Once you take your skates off after skating for a while, you feel like you're moving faster than you are. This sensation can make you dizzy. The solution is to keep walking. If you stop and focus on the sensation of moving you will make it worse. The mind must be renewed.

Our mind works much the same way when it comes to understanding spiritual truth. When the Holy Spirit comes with conviction it takes a while for our natural mind to catch up. If we focus on the sin and try to change ourselves we will only make it worse. Jesus does not ask us to die to sin, He did that. He asks us to die to self. Self must move out of the way.

The pattern of the world is self-discipline, which focuses on self effort. The Bible tells us to be self-controlled (Galatians 5:23), which means self is controlled by the Spirit. The focus is on the Spirit. In order for the Spirit to truly be in control of us we must have what I call a "Damascus Road experience." In Acts 9, Saul (who later is known as Paul), gets knocked off his high horse and comes face to face with the Lordship of Jesus Christ.

Let me tell you about my Damascus experience. It was New Years Eve and I could not find anything to fit me! I had struggled with my weight for years. I begged God to help me, but nothing worked. So, I was depressed and angry. I cried out to God in desperation that night. I told God I had reached the end of my rope.

Usually, when I would feel this badly I could quote enough scripture to get myself up, but not this time. I was tired. I was so tired that I felt like I might give up on God completely. So, I said, "God if You want me to be saved, You are going to have to do something, because I can't."

Up until that point the word *can't* was a four letter word to me. The Bible says, "I can do all things through Christ," so I thought lightning might strike me dead. I expected God to be angry with me. Instead, I heard God say, "Finally."

I was shocked. Finally, God was able to help me, because I couldn't get back up on my high horse this time. I came face to face with the reality that God—and only God—was the power in my life. Paul tells us in II Corinthians 12:9 that God's power is perfected in our weakness.

Each of us must encounter God in a similar way. Many Christians only know intellectually that God is in control. However, we must experience this truth in order for it to be true in our lives. I cannot tell you how to have this experience. I can tell you that if you have, you know it and can describe exactly what happened to you.

So, if you cannot describe a Damascus Road experience in your life then start praying that you will have one. I can guarantee it will not be fun. Dying is never fun. I can promise you that it will change your life and usher you into a whole new level of relationship with God. Coming to the realization that God is in control and that we only have the right to obey and trust Him is what it means to "deny self." Once we die to self then the Holy Spirit is able to control our lives.

How does the Holy Spirit control us? We must keep walking in the truth so the mind can be renewed. Stay focused on God, not your sin. Let the Holy Spirit show you why He has brought conviction into your life. Then trust God to transform you as you continue to seek Him in prayer and devotion. This is a huge adjustment to our religious thinking. Religion puts the emphasis on us, not God. To deny yourself is not about self discipline; it is about self dying.

Do not play the role of the Holy Spirit. As a pastor, I have a great burden to help people grow in their relationship with God. Even before I answered the call to full-time ministry these gifts were evident in my life. As a teenager my friends were always asking me for advice. As a result, I developed an expectation for myself; I had to have the answers for people.

For a long time I thought this was my responsibility as a pastor. I know I'm not the only one living under this burden. Then one day the Holy Spirit led me to John 14. In this chapter Jesus is telling His disciples that He must go away and when He does the Holy Spirit will come. As I was reading this passage Jesus asked me, "If I knew I couldn't do the work of the Holy Spirit what makes you so sure you can?" That one question has totally revolutionized my ministry and my life.

I began to realize that it was not my job to convict people of wrong, it was not my job to get them to do the right things. It is my job to reconcile people to God so the Holy Spirit can do the convicting (II Corinthians 5:18).

This principle also applies to our own lives as well. We cannot be the Holy Spirit and we must not allow others to be the Holy Spirit in our lives. If we do, we will develop unsanctified convictions that will serve as bondage rather than liberty in our lives. If I do the right thing for the wrong reason it can distract me from God.

Let me give you an example of an unsanctified conviction. When I was younger my father had a conviction about going to movie theaters. Consequently, I took this conviction on as my own. However, every time I was confronted with an opportunity to go to the theater I would become frustrated. I felt confined and unable to explain why it was wrong, it just was.

Then one day I was confronted with a question that made my conviction seem hypocritical. I was asked, "Why do you go into video stores then? Isn't it the same thing?"

Since the conviction I was carrying came from my father and not the Lord, I had no reply. Finally, I went to the Lord about it. Why was I frustrated about this conviction? Most of my other convictions brought liberty and safety into my life, not frustration. The Lord showed me that He was not able to convict me in this area because I assumed someone else's conviction. Since the conviction was not God's it was not producing sanctification in my life. The result of an unsanctified conviction is confinement and frustration.

So, I let go of my father's conviction and let the Lord give me my own. I encourage you to make sure no one plays the Holy Spirit in your life and do not try to be Him for others. The goal is not a lifestyle but a relationship. Even if we have good convictions and a clean life before God, it doesn't mean we know Him. These are the types of things we must deny in our lives in order to follow Jesus.

Paul was desperate to die. He wanted nothing short of an intimate relationship with Jesus.

"I want to know Christ and the power of His resurrection and the fellowship of sharing in his sufferings, becoming like Him in His death and so, some how, to attain to the resurrection from the dead."

Philippians 3:10

The struggle with dying to self is in giving up the right to our own opinion.

The surprise comes in discovering the freedom and simplicity of God's ways.

Let us die to self, let us deny our rights, for the rewards are far greater than the sacrifice.

Let's be desperate to die!

Notes

6

Trying Truth

The Bible says, "the truth shall set you free. So, why do we run from it?

The carnal nature fears truth. That is why we never have to teach our children to lie, it comes naturally.

> *"Everyone who does evil hates the light, and will not come into the light for fear that his deeds will be exposed. But whoever lives by the truth comes into the light, so that it may be seen plainly that what he has done has been done through God."*
>
> *John 3:20, 21*

Fear is the gateway into Satan's domain. He uses fear to trap us in his ways. We have all been in a situation where fear prevented us from being truthful. Then it took another lie to cover up the first one. Before you knew it, the situation was out of control.

In my house, lying is the one thing that invokes the wrath of mom! In order to avoid this hardship we have established a few rules.

Rule #1: Lying will always get you double the punishment of whatever you are trying to hide.

Rule #2: If you are afraid to confess something because mom and dad might get angry, then say, "I have a special secret."

As parents, my husband and I have agreed not to get angry when our children confess their sin. Like our heavenly Father we want our children to learn that the truth is easier to deal with than a lie. We are trying to eliminate the fear of telling the truth for our children. God wants to eliminate this fear in his children too.

As long as we fear the truth, Satan can use it against us. But if we are willing to be truthful, he has no hold over us. Only we can take back what the enemy has stolen by confessing the truth.

The fact is, when we hide from the truth we are only fooling ourselves. Doesn't it drive you crazy when someone makes excuses for their mistakes rather than just admitting them? I know I have much more respect for someone when they just say, "I was wrong."

When I was a kid I drove my father crazy with all the excuses I had for why I did things. I just wanted him know why I did what I did. Quite simply, people don't care why, they just need to know that we know we were wrong. God is the same way. We must learn to embrace the truth rather than fear it.

The Struggle

"God is light; in him there is no darkness at all. If we claim to have fellowship with him yet walk in the darkness, we lie and do not live by the truth. But if we walk in the light as he is in the light, we have fellowship with one another and the blood of Jesus purifies us from all sin."

I John 1:5-8

Light is synonymous with the truth in scripture. Deception is darkness which is the opposite of truth. Deception is trying to present ourselves in the best possible light. Webster defines deception as illusion. According to I John, if we deceive people we are not in right relationship with God. It is like the guy late for work who tries to come up with a good excuse to tell his boss. He is trying to create an illusion, which is deception. Telling the truth in this situation requires admittance of failure. Many people refuse to admit failure in order to "save face."

Fear is the gateway into Satan's domain.

According to I John 1:5-9 when we walk in the truth we have fellowship with each other. So, admitting failure and apologizing would be better for us than if we deceive by making up an excuse!

Being truthful becomes even harder when there is more at stake. Like the wife who doesn't want to admit to her husband that she maxed out the credit card. Instead she starts blaming him for not having a good enough job. Or the husband who fails at hiding his mistress, so he tells his wife she is a business associate.

Deception is just an attempt at making ourselves look as good as we can in our present situation. Fear of exposure keeps us from admitting the truth. We make the mistake of thinking deception will protect us. If only this theory worked. Even if people believe our lies we still lose.

Satan will always remind you what it costs to obey God, but will never tell you the cost of disobeying. Disobedience is always more costly!

Why does deception fail every time? God has certain laws in place that prevent deception from being successful. One of these laws is the law of the harvest. This law states that *we reap what we sow* (Galatians 6:7). If I deceive, I too will be deceived. What goes around comes around.

When I was first married I had a leased vehicle. During the duration of the lease, my windshield was cracked just below the windshield wipers. It was not clearly visible. When we turned in the car, the inspector did not notice the crack.

Several weeks later he called to ask if the crack was there when we turned in the car. I asked if he saw it when he inspected the car. He replied no. I said, "Isn't it your job to find the crack?"

Wow! What deception that was. He hung up the phone and we were not charged for the crack. However, when we turned in the *next* car lease we were charged double what that windshield would have cost. The charges were for marks made by the previous owner that the inspector forgot to include in our lease! Deception does not pay!

The truth is always easier to deal with than the lie! Keep in mind that the cost for deception may not be related to the same type of problem, as in the illustration of my car. Maybe the price to pay is your children having to find another job out of town and you can not be with your grandchildren. It may take a deep soul search by the Holy Spirit to show you what bad fruit you are harvesting through disobedience.

A second law that hinders deception from being successful is found in Matthew 7:2. This law teaches us that, "to the measure we use it will be measured back to us." One thing about human nature is that we expect others to give us mercy, but we want justice when we have been wronged.

This imbalanced thinking allows us to justify our own actions while condemning the actions of others. So, when we are confronted with our own wrong actions we make excuses, yet when confronting the actions of someone else we refuse excuses.

What we need to realize is that we are going to receive from others what we give. For instance, most people who are deceptive are also mistrustful. Why? Because they expect others to be as they are. The fear of being deceived and mistrusting others is a terrible burden. This is the reward of deception!

Let's have a

SoulSOAK

Still your mind • Open your heart • Affirm God's truth • Kindle new passion

The Blessing

We will walk in the light as Jesus is in the light. We will live honestly with God and man. We will not practice deception. Instead, we will be lovers of the truth.

The Meditation

1. In what ways have you practiced deception?

2. Ask the Holy Spirit to reveal any area of your life that you may be reaping from deception or disobedience. Now, ask the Holy Spirit what must be done to resolve it.

The Prayer

Holy Spirit I know that you want to protect me and present me blameless to the Father. I open my heart to your probing. Reveal whatever deception may be lurking there that I am unaware of. I am committed to walk in the truth so lead the way. Starting today I will…

The enemy will always remind us what it will cost us to obey God, but he will never tell us what it will cost to disobey. The truth can be a heavy burden to confess, but it is much heavier to conceal. If you are carrying the burden of secret sin, James instructs us to confess our sins one to another that we might be healed.

If your sin is against someone else, seek council with your pastor or spiritual advisor. Let them help you confess your sin in the most beneficial way for all who are involved. Remember, the truth will set you free (See John 8:32).

The Surprise

Deceiving yourself is the biggest deception of them all. The reality is that we do not know what we do not know! Many Christians are walking around convinced that they understand God's ways, but they have no idea that they do not. Spiritual pride has blinded them to the truth. They are living in self deception. Even you, reading this book right now, might be totally unaware that you are deceived by pride. It is a scary–but very real–possibility.

The scriptures teach us that the truth sets us free (John 8:32). We cannot be free until we know the truth. The truth is not so scary when we realize God will not use it against us.

We sometimes are afraid to be truthful with God because we fear exposure or we do not want to fail him. As long as we remain engaged in the process of change we will not fail God. God knows we are not perfect. He is not shaken by our sin or failures. It is not perfection, but honesty that God seeks (I John 1:7). If we keep running from the truth we will remain in deception.

So, how do we discover the truth, if we are blinded by self deception?

James 4:6 says, "God opposes the proud but gives grace to the humble." The Lord gave me a vision to help me understand this principle better. I saw a small little clown with torn clothes and a dirty face walking merrily along. Attached to the back of this clown was a large hook. As the clown walked across my view the hook latched on to a giant screen that rolled back as he walked. Even though the clown was unaware of what was happening, he was exposing the entire universe that was hidden behind the screen.

As I experienced this vision, I was thinking to myself, "Why was this unimportant little clown given the honor of revealing the universe? He did not even know what he was doing." The Lord read my thoughts and replied with James 4:6. The clown represented humility. If we are humble God will grace us with spiritual understanding. The way he opposes the proud is by letting them remain blind. God will not fight for the right to be understood. We either gain access into God's truth through humility or we will remain deceived and not even know it!

Remember, our brain does not have the capacity to tell us the information we have stored could be wrong. This is why humility is so important. We must train ourselves to admit wrong and search out truth. We must never dismiss something as wrong just because we have different information stored in our brain. If we do that, we will never discover self deception in our life! What a waste that would be as God desires to reveal the universe to us. No matter how long we have walked with God, we are always just beginning to know the infinite Creator.

Do not allow pride to keep you from all that God desires to reveal in your life! He is an awesome God and wants fellowship with us! All we have to do is walk truthfully before Him.

Humility is the first step to discovering the truth. The second is council. Proverbs 1:5 says, "Let the wise listen and add to their learning, and let the discerning get guidance." We all have blind spots in our lives. We can see the blind spot in others, but never in ourselves. We observe others and think to ourselves, "Can't they see how silly they look?" The surprise is, others are doing that to us as well. If we are wise and courageous enough we will seek the council of someone we trust to reveal our blind spots. Remember, when someone is revealing your blind spot to you, you will probably disagree. We must take this information before the Lord to receive the revelation we need.

Third, and most important, it takes the fear of the Lord to discover the truth (Proverbs 1:7). Unless we have a passion to please God we will not care about the truth. A person who does not fear God is wise in his own eyes (Proverbs 3:7). God is not going to run after the fool. He will allow him to go on thinking that he is right until it is too late! Do not be a fool! Humble yourself. Seek council. Fear God and learn the truth!

The struggle in being truthful is that we do not want to admit failure and are afraid of rejection.

The surprise in being truthful is that God is not interested in exposing us as failures. Rather God desires to reveal himself to those who walk honestly before Him.

Notes

7

Poised for Prayer

We can never be prayer warriors until we see prayer as the most effective way to enable change.

I remember asking a pastor once how much we should pray every day. His answer was, "Until you are through." The key to a productive prayer life is intimacy with God. If you do not know God very well then you will not have a strong desire to communicate with Him. If you are intimate with God, then you know He is the one who initiates our prayer life.

In Luke 4, Jesus is led into the wilderness by the Holy Spirit to pray and fast. Isaiah 56:7 says, "These I will bring to My holy mountain and give them joy in My house of prayer." In other words, God causes us to pray. For example, a sleepless night can be an indication that God wants to spend some time with us. Instead of tossing and turning or taking a sleeping pill, we should pray. We need to ask God if He has awoken us.

Someone may come to your mind that you have not thought of in years, or maybe a particular situation is weighing heavy on your mind. This is God wanting us to pray. So often we fail to recognize the Holy Spirit leading us into prayer. Did you ever have a dream about someone you have not seen in a long time, only to see that person a few days later? This is not a coincidence. We must become more aware of the Holy Spirit trying to prepare us for His divine appointments.

The next time someone just pops into your head for no reason, ask the Holy Spirit why you should pray for them. Then, if you see them you will be more prepared, should God lead you to minister to them.

If God initiates prayer why do we feel so guilty about not praying enough? Guilt is usually the motivator when it comes to prayer. Many Christians have been made to feel like they are huge sinners if they do not come to all the prayer meetings in the church. As an intercessor, I know how passionate prayer teams can be about their prayer meetings. Unfortunately, guilt and manipulation are not very effective ways to help someone build a prayer life. Trust me, I've tried it! If prayer is out of obligation rather than passion it will not be very productive.

Another reason people do not pray enough is because it is boring! Don't be shocked that I said it. We cannot overcome what we cannot admit. So, why is prayer boring? It is boring only when man is in charge of it. Humanity thinks prayer needs to be hard, silent, and repetitive. All of these ideas come from the lack of a good prayer language. Most Christians run out of things to say in the first ten minutes. This is because we haven't learned to ask Jesus what He prays about.

Hebrews tells us that Jesus is our great High Priest. He is always making intercession before the throne of God on our behalf. We should be asking Jesus what He is praying for. He hasn't run out of things to say in over two thousand years. Once you let Jesus lead your prayer life it won't be boring. Beware, if Jesus is telling you how to pray, it probably won't be what you wanted to pray, or how you wanted to pray. Be open to God's guidance stretching you.

We must get out of our comfort zone and trust Jesus to keep us "balanced." Everybody is so worried about balance. The fact is, we are so out of balance with the Word when it comes to prayer. The way I read it, I'm supposed to move mountains! Until my prayers are producing biblical results, I'm going to assume I do not know enough about prayer to be an expert on how it's done! I'm going to keep letting Jesus lead me.

If prayer is out of obligation rather than passion it will not be very effective.

For example, several years ago I was at a church meeting involving several churches from the area. I was asked to organize and lead the intercessors from the different churches in prayer several hours before the meeting. Our prayer team was accustomed to using flags and banners during prayer, but not everyone who came to pray that night prayed in the same way. I was going to do the polite thing and not use the flags, but God had other plans.

The Lord told me to have all the men take red flags and wave them violently like a weapon in front of all the doorways. This was not exactly appreciated as a legitimate form of prayer by many of the men. Many of them did not understand what I was up to until later in the evening. I think many of them thought I was crazy.

As long as we depend more on ourselves than prayer we will have a weak prayer life. As long as we think prayer helps us do the job, we will be in God's way.

However, later that night the guest speaker spoke on the Passover. He told us it was the Jewish custom for the men to cover their doorways with blood to protect their families. The speaker used the Passover as an analogy of how Christian men needed to do battle against the enemy and not allow the devil to attack their families. The Lord led the intercessors to wave the red flags over the doorways of the church to spiritually prepare for the message that night. I had no idea what the message was going to be about, I just allowed the Holy Spirit to direct our prayer time even though it was somewhat inconvenient to do what he was telling me to do.

Let us remember that the God we serve paints the sky red, shines a rainbow when it storms, and has variety of every kind set in perfect order. This is not the picture of a boring God. It is not compatible with the character of God to have everything explainable and predictable. He's the one who made the bee fly even though it is aerodynamically impossible. I think He did that just to keep us guessing. Let us not be so certain we know how God does things! It is amazing what we can learn when we let this wonderful, creative God do the praying through us.

If you want to have a better prayer life, let go of the guilt and let God carry you away with Him into His world. That can happen anytime, anywhere, no matter what you're doing, so get poised for prayer!

The Struggle

Prayer is not a tool that helps us do God's work. Prayer is God's work. Unless prayer is the first thing we do, it will not have the power God intended it to have in our lives. Prayer should not be the last resort when all of our own plans fail.

Prayer is the most effective way to enable change. All too often we hinder, sidestep, derail or even stop what God is trying to do for us because we have not gone to Him in prayer.

In the early years of the ministry I tried to "help" God do His work. So when I saw someone who needed "guidance" they got it, even if they did not want it. I called this type of spiritual manipulation "discipleship." Then one day I was reading Ezekiel 22:30, which says, "I looked for a man among them who would build up the wall and stand before me in the gap on behalf of the land..."

I thought the Lord directed me to that passage to thank me for being that person. I surely was standing in the gap between God and man! The Lord showed me that I was facing the wrong way in the gap. The scripture asks for someone to stand in the gap before God, not before man. I was facing man rather than facing God. So, when God would show me something, instead of praying for Him to intervene, I would intervene. God does not want us doing His job. He wants us to pray so the Holy Spirit can do the job. If we are going to see the power of prayer in our lives it must become to us the most effective way to enable change.

How does this change in perspective happen? It happens in our thought life first. We all have times of the day when our mind is free to ponder useless things. When we are driving in our car or washing dishes or taking a shower, these are perfect opportunities to pray.

I used to use these times to think about how I was going to solve certain problems. I would have conversations with people in my head, imagining what I would say if I had the opportunity. Those conversations were often critical of others. Most of us would admit to having similar experiences with our thought life. However, this type of thinking is very draining and has a great effect on our disposition and even our character. Romans 12 teaches us that we are spiritually transformed by the renewing of our mind.

Our thoughts control our behavior. It is far more productive and energy-producing to use our thought life as prayer time. Instead of arguing with someone in your head, pray for them. Instead of wrestling with the pro and con game, trying to surmise the will of God by deduction, pray. When Paul urges us in Philippians to pray without ceasing, he did not mean do nothing else with your life. Praying without ceasing means that you have an attitude of prayer throughout your day. If someone offends you, do not relive the offense over and over in your mind. Pray for that individual to realize what they have done. Ask God to help you forgive. We must learn to turn our thought life into prayer time.

Once I began to pray instead of react to the things around me God began to change them. I would see people begin to understand the very things I was praying about for them. I was shocked to realize the Holy Spirit didn't need my help, just my prayers. This is not easy, but very rewarding. When we take our hands off of the situation it frees God to do his work, as we pray.

Years ago I was very burdened for a family member that was turning away from God. One day while in prayer God showed me what I needed to do for this person. I saw him in my mind's eye struggling with a huge black spider on his back. Then I saw myself running up to him, I was trying to help him remove the spider. As we were wrestling, he began to fight me as well. Then I saw the whole vision start all over again. This time instead of helping him, I got down on my knees and prayed. As I was praying this man began to gain the strength to fight the spider himself. God spoke to me at that moment and told me not to speak another word to this person about God until further notice.

Fifteen years passed, I prayed and prayed, but never spoke a word to him about the Lord. Finally, the Lord released me to share with him again, only after he had returned to the Lord. I know that if I had not obeyed I would have affected my relationship with my family in a negative way. We must learn that prayer is the most effective way to enable change.

The hardest thing to do is to watch people suffer because they will not turn to God or obey His word. It is very challenging to treat people as God does—by giving them the right to fail. Sometimes our desire to protect people turns into control and manipulation. We must have enough grace to back away and let people learn on their own—but not too far off that they can't reach out to us if they want. Praying, instead of reacting, tries our patience and faith in God. If you want to fellowship in the suffering of Christ try it. Can you image how painful it must be to God when He allows us to fail, and we blame Him afterwards?

Why is prayer the most effective way to enable change? If we try to fix things ourselves we usually get in God's way. For instance, the pain we try to protect people from is usually what God uses to help them. The classic enabler is a good example of this. The parent of an alcoholic child hires the best lawyer to beat the rap and thinks they have helped their child. Only later on, the child kills someone in a car accident. We often try to get people out of trouble. God is the One who let them get into it in the first place. If we pray instead of react, we allow God to show us His plan. Often God will use us to help people, but it usually is not in the way we might expect.

The pain we try to protect people from is usually what God uses to help them. If we pray instead of react we allow God to show His plan.

Another reason prayer is the most effective way to see things change is because of "spiritual fornication." What is that? "Spiritual fornication" is a term God gave me to help me learn to pray, rather than responding to my situation.

Fornication is when people are intimate with each other before they have made the commitment of marriage. Spiritual fornication is when people receive from others what God alone wanted to reveal to them. God wants to develop an intimate relationship with each of us. When we are focused on people instead of God, we give away His secrets and steal the opportunity for others to learn from Him directly.

When I was in high school I had a huge crush on the biggest flirt in the school. He was not a Christian and I was. My parents could have easily forbidden me to date him because they wanted to protect me. Instead, my father sat me down and said, "Joy, you are free to make your own decision about this boy. Just know that if you choose to dishonor God you will not be able to live under this roof." It wasn't long before this boy gave me an ultimatum. He told me it hurt him too badly to date me if he couldn't "be with me!" What a line that was! I looked him in the eye and told him it was his loss, not mine. I felt so good after that. God showed me that I was too special to just give myself away. If my parents had intervened that would have kept me pure too, at least in that situation. However, I would have resented my parents for controlling me and missed out on the intimate time with the Lord. By the way, that intimate experience with God kept me pure until I married at age twenty nine!

I know now just how hard it must have been for my parents to let me figure things out on my own. They told me later that they spent many nights on their knees for their kids. I really do not think my relationship with God would be as strong as it is today if my parents hadn't prayed instead of interfered in my life.

If we learn to pray first in every situation, we will receive God's wisdom as His ways are revealed to us. Of course, there are times that we must intervene. Jude 23 tells us to snatch some from the fire–which means that some people need intervention. Please do not hear me say our lives are just about prayer. However, more often than not we probably err for not praying, rather than only praying.

The Surprise

If we are going to pray we want God to answer us. We know God wants to answer our prayers and yet so often it appears as though he does not. Many of us have been told that God answers prayer in one of three ways: yes, no or wait. It may come as a surprise to hear that there is not much proof of that in scripture.

This is the confidence we have in approaching God: that if we ask anything according to his will, he hears us. And if we know that he hears us- whatever we ask- we know that we have what we asked of Him.

I John 5:14

According to this passage, God only hears us if we are asking what He wants us to ask for. Our confidence comes in knowing that we have been heard—not answered! We have the responsibility to find out how God wants us to pray and if we do not do that, God does not even hear us. Our prayers are a waste of time if we are praying according to our own plans and ideas.

So, I guess it is pretty pointless to keep asking for something over and over again. According to this scripture, if it wasn't right the first time, God isn't even listening! If I John 5:14 hasn't convinced you, how about what Jesus says here?

If you remain in Me and My words remain in you, ask whatever you wish, and it will be given you.

John 15:7

Nothing here in this passage is about God saying "no" or even "wait." The key is in remaining in God. If we remain in God, our wishes will be

His wishes and that is why He will always answer "yes" to our prayers. James 4:3 tells us that we do not get what we ask for because we ask in the wrong way. In each one of these scriptures, God does not make Himself the heavy by saying "no" or "not now" to our requests. Instead he allows us the opportunity to hear "yes" every time. All we have to do is be intimate with God. When we know God, we know what we should ask for and when and how to ask for it! Now that is true power!

This may be a good time to close the book and spend sometime with God about this subject. I can imagine that what I have just said may not be easy for you, because it wasn't easy for me. I may not understand it all, but God does. Let Him sort it out for you. Just be open to the Holy Spirit and allow Him to lead you into truth.

So, how do we develop a "Yes" prayer life?

Ask and it will be given to you; seek and you will find;
knock and the door will be opened to you.

Matthew 7:7

This passage will unlock the key to intimacy with God and access to God's power. This is the "Ask, Seek, Knock model" for the "Yes" prayer life.

Step One: Ask

If you are asking for something and you are not getting it, stop asking for it! If you are asking for the right thing then you will get it. If you are not getting it, you're not asking for the right thing. You can beg, plead, scream, cry, fast or stand on your head. It will not matter, because you are not being heard!

I know this is hard to hear, but hang in there with me, it gets better. If you are being heard, you will get what you ask for. I remember when God was teaching me this principle I asked Him about the Syrophoenician woman (see Mark 7:24-30) and the persistent friend begging for bread (see Luke 11:5-8). These two people kept asking until they got what they wanted. These parables demonstrate the heart of desperation a true prayer warrior has before God. However, many ask with a heart that is spoiled and demanding. Desperation is what moves the heart of God.

Step Two: Seek

If you have been asking for something and have not gotten it, that is your cue to move on to step two. We must begin to seek God for the answer. Why am I not getting what I have asked for? God wants us to discover Him. If we lay down our own desires to hear Him speak, we will have open communication again.

During worship one Sunday morning God showed me how to seek Him. I saw myself in a wooded area franticly searching for my lost daughter. I was calling out her name as I desperately pulled back leaves and branches to reveal what was ahead. I had completely abandoned what I had come to the woods for in the first place. All that mattered now was that I find my daughter.

The Lord spoke to me and said, "Unless you seek me in this same manner you will not find me." Next, I saw myself at the kitchen sink doing dishes. I was calling out for my daughter again, only this time I was expecting her to come to me. I had no intention of leaving what I was doing to go find her. Then the Lord said, "This is how most of my children seek me."

When we say we are seeking the Lord we must abandon all of our own desires and ways of thinking first. Discovering how God feels is what should be most important, not trying to get God to see it our way. Once we learn this abandonment and God can trust us to hold His heart, then we will be ready for the next step.

Step Three: Knock

Step two is the most agonizing and glorious place to be in God. The adventure of discovering the heart of God is spectacular. The glory of knowing God is worth the pain of abandonment. But abandonment is the price we pay for discovering God. We will have our hearts torn out and bang our heads against the wall trying to discover Him. Oh, but what joy we will share when we do, at last, find God.

This, of course, is an ongoing adventure of seek and discovery until we come to the place of unity with God. This is a place only those who have known it can talk about. Just keep seeking God until you get there. When you do you will know. This place of unity with Christ is about seeing all the doors in front of you, but only knocking on the one that will open. Jesus had this unity with the Father. He said that He only does that He sees His father doing (see John 5:19).

Jesus saw His father at work when he walked up to just one man at the pool of Bethesda (see John 5:2). It does not say Jesus healed any of the others that were there that day. He saw all the opportunities to heal, but he only knocked on the door that would open. When it comes to healing, Isaiah 53:5 says, "by His stripes we are healed." That creates many doors of opportunity for us. We must be united with Christ to knock only on the doors that will open to us. This is the key to a "Yes" prayer life.

We must learn that prayer is the most effective way to enable change.

The struggle with having a good prayer life is learning to pray before we react to our situation.

It is surprising to realize that prayer is not about God coming to our aid, but about us going after God.

Notes

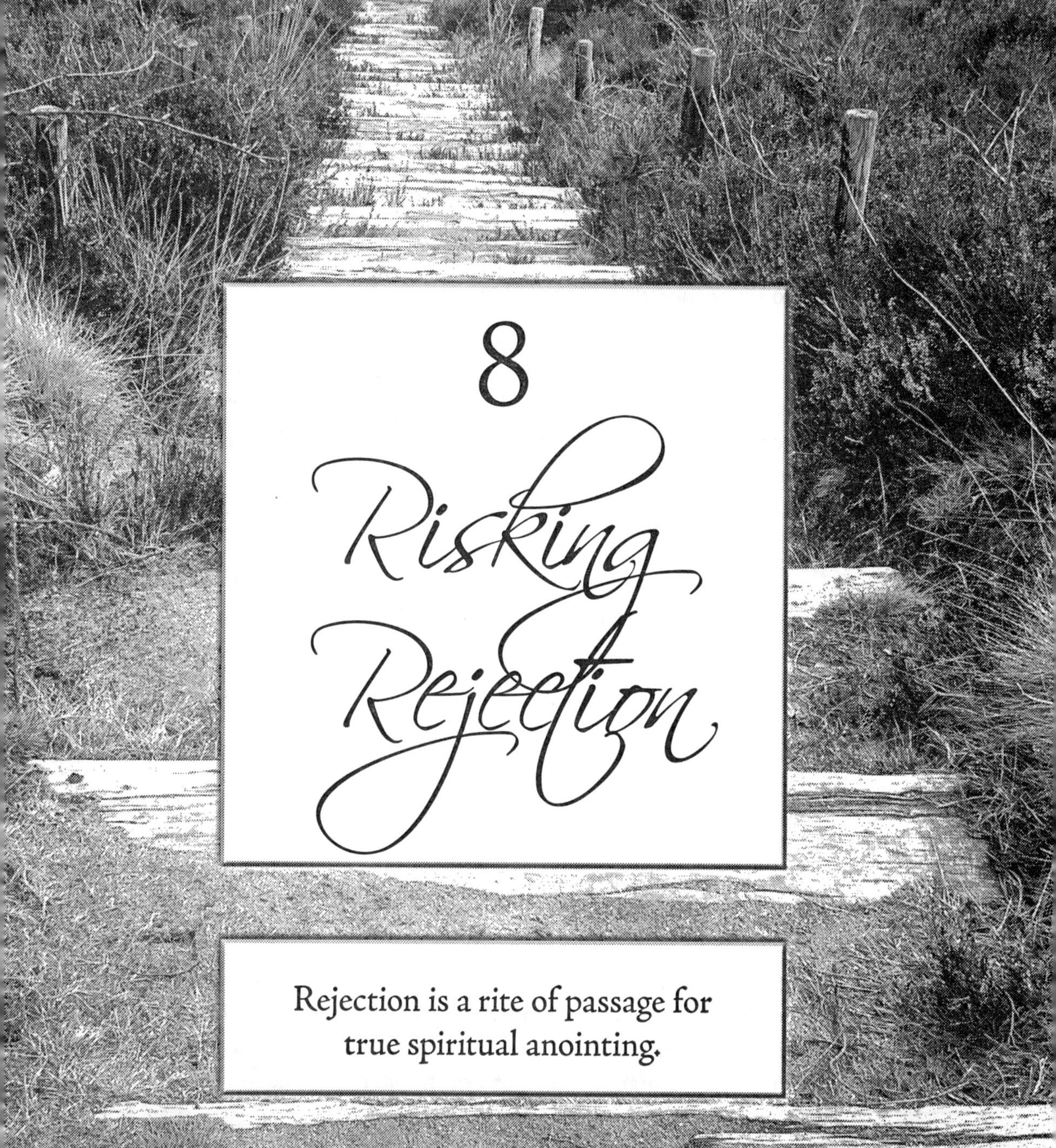

8

Risking Rejection

Rejection is a rite of passage for true spiritual anointing.

To feel like we belong and are accepted by our peers is a fundamental human need. We have been created for love, because of love, and to love. This is why rejection can be the most devastating human emotion. Rejection has caused our kids to cry, our teens to kill and our leaders to go to war! So, why would God cause us to risk rejection in order to experience ultimate love and power?

Rejection is a rite of passage. A rite of passage is a turning point. It marks the passage from one level of maturity to another. If we are going to experience God's intended divine love we must rid ourselves of all other forms of inferior love. God's love is unconditional (John 4:16-19). Human love is conditional. Conditional love says, "I love you if, I love you when, I love you because." It is because of our inferior love that humans face rejection.

Do not love the world or anything in the world. If anyone loves the world, the love of the Father is not in him. For everything in the world—the cravings of sinful man, the lust of his eyes and the boasting of what he has and does—comes not from the Father but from the world. The world and its desires pass away, but the man who does the will of God lives forever.

I John 2:15-17

We need to examine this passage closely. First, take a look at what the world is comprised of: the cravings of sinful man, the lust of his eyes and the pride in his heart. It is the world that produces these horrible things in us. How does the world do that? The world has a basis of acceptance that is rooted in conditions. These conditions produce our value system.

For instance, if my basis of acceptance is rooted in the condition of wealth then I would be materialistic. This value system of materialism can cause me to desire all sorts of sinful things. I might start gambling in order to maintain the level of wealth that makes me feel accepted. I could sell drugs or maybe become a workaholic. That is why this passage tells me I cannot love the world and have God's love too. As long as my acceptance is based upon conditions, I will not know God's unconditional love.

Many Christians are very worldly even though they do not do worldly things. For instance, if your basis of acceptance is rooted in meeting Christian criteria then you are loving the world. God does not accept us on the basis of meeting certain Christian criteria. That is worldly love with a twist of Christianity. It is religious and deadly!

As long as we feel accepted only when we meet certain conditions, we are worldly. This passage in I John states that the world and its desires are passing away. The criteria for acceptance are always changing. As long as we are worldly we will never really feel accepted because the world is always changing what it wants from us.

Oh, but God… What a glorious phrase. God does not want us to settle for conditional love. He wants to envelope us in the all consuming power of His unconditional love. Imagine just letting go of all the expectations and demands placed on you. Imagine just reveling in the fact that you are loved, right now, just as you are. Many Christians sadly say they "know" God loves them unconditionally but their worldly heart has never allowed them to feel it! God wants you to feel His love, rest in it and be compelled by it. That is why God must rid us of all the forms of inferior love that keep us from experiencing His love.

If we will embrace rejection as an opportunity to be cleansed from worldly love, then we will grow in God's grace and love. If we keep responding to the rejection with defensiveness or anger then we remain trapped in the world's system of conditional love. If we allow ourselves to be influenced by the conditions of worldly acceptance then we stay trapped as well. Galatians 5:1 tells us that we have been freed by the blood of Jesus

Christ, and we must not allow ourselves to be put back under the yoke of slavery. Risk rejection and become free from conditional love!

Let's have a

SoulSOAK

Still your mind • Open your heart • Affirm God's truth • Kindle new passion

The Blessing

Over you is divine love, like a banner it hails the truth that you are the beloved of God's. There is nothing you can do to earn this position and nothing can separate you from it (Romans 8:38-39). You will walk confidently in this truth and will not bow to the world's conditions for acceptance. Rejection will not be feared but expected, knowing that you are not of this world nor will you be understood by it.

The Meditation

1. List at least three experiences from your past that left you feeling rejected. Ask the Holy Spirit if these experiences have left a negative impression on you. If So, ask Him to touch your heart with His love and heal the rejection.

2. Do you have worldly love? If so, what are the conditions you feel you must meet to be accepted? Do you hold others to these same conditions? If you want to be free, repent and ask God to cleanse you from worldly love. Keep in mind, He may use rejection to do it.

The Prayer

Lord, forgive me for any worldliness in me. I want to receive your unconditional love and I want to love others unconditionally. Help me to let go of the pain of past rejection. I do not want to fear it any more. Instead, I want to embrace it and allow it to cleanse me from inferior love. Starting today I will…

The Struggle

I remember sitting in the audience during a conference at which I was one of the speakers. The man preaching began to teach on the scripture we've been talking about in I John. Keep in mind that I was already a pastor and conference speaker at that time. The Holy Spirit revealed to me that I could preach about His love, but I had never truly felt loved by God. I realized at that moment that I was trying to earn God's love, even though I knew the scriptures told me God loved me while I was yet a sinner (see Romans 5:8).

I opened my heart to the Lord that day in a way I have never done before. I felt the love of God flood my soul. He embraced me with all my weaknesses and failures and I knew I was loved. I know some of you reading this think you know what I am talking about. Just like I thought I knew what I was preaching about. Let me just say, there is a difference between knowing something intellectually and knowing it through experience. God does not want us to know about His love, he wants us to experience it, to feel it, to be governed by it.

Many of us have been wounded so deeply that we receive help as criticism and a difference of opinion as rejection.

For instance, I can know God's love forgives, but does His forgiveness govern me when I need to be forgiving? If we struggle to forgive others, we have not truly experienced God's forgiveness. We may know about God's love, but we have not experienced it. When we have experienced the freedom and power of being forgiven it enables us to forgive others. Remember, those who are forgiven much love much (Luke 7:47).

God wants us to be empowered by His forgiveness so we can be free to forgive. If you need to feel God's forgiveness in your life, then pray this prayer with me:

Father, I know that your Son, Jesus, has done all that needs to be done. I know that His death and resurrection is more than enough to pay for all the wrong I have committed against you and others. I need to be free from my worldly heart, that I might really experience all that I know to be true about Your love and forgiveness.

I am tired from carrying guilt and allowing myself to feel responsible to fix the wrong. I humbly acknowledge that I cannot fix the wrong or make up for the failure in my life. Please, release me from the conditions I place on myself that do not come from You. Set me free from the expectations of others. I want to feel forgiven and I want to be able to forgive others.

Empower me by Your grace to live free from sin and shame.

If you need God to answer this prayer for you today then close the book and spend some time with Jesus. Let His presence wash over you and cleanse you from all the guilt and shame that has been weighing you down.

A wounded spirit prevents us from receiving our "inheritance in the saints" (Ephesians 1:18). God has devised an awesome plan of perpetual blessing which is poured out among his children. We must learn to appreciate the differences among us and work together instead of competing with each other. We all have different gifts. These gifts enable us to view life from different vantage points. If we are willing to humble ourselves and risk rejection, we will discover the joy of unity in Christ.

When the different gifts are permitted to function together they cause the body to depend on each other. For instance, a pastor needs godly intercessors who will watch his back. However, many pastors have been wounded by controlling sheep who think they should tell the pastor what to do. So, instead of the pastor benefiting from the care and protection of godly intercessors, he avoids anyone who says, "God wants me to pray for you." This problem is apparent for two reasons. First, some intercessors do not understand the limits of their authority. Second, some pastors are too insecure to rely on members of their congregation.

The devil easily causes division in the church because we do not understand one another's gifts. As a result, most Christians are hesitant to be honest among other Christians. Instead, we try to say and do all the "right things," we are too afraid to be ourselves.

This includes leadership. I was actually taught that, as a leader, I should not share my weaknesses with my congregation. I was told, "familiarity breeds contempt," and it is true in some cases. But I refuse to be a phony just because some people will abuse me for being honest. If the apostle Paul can boast in his weaknesses, so can I (see II Corinthians 12:9).

We cannot settle for soulish power, which can build big churches but not powerful Christians.

I also want to be able to say like Paul, follow me as I follow Christ (see I Corinthians 11:1). If I refuse to let people see me struggle in my walk with the Lord, then how can they follow me? As leaders, what are we really teaching people if all we ever talk about is the victories? Come on! We all know we are not always successful. We struggle just like everyone else to hear God's voice. We even struggle with obedience. How dare we mislead people about who we really are? More importantly, how dare we lead people to believe they cannot know God like we do because we're so "holy?" Shepherds lead from in front of the flock. We should be saying, "Watch how God helps me when I struggle. Now you do the same."

Instead, we often act like cowboys, whipping our flocks as we drive them from behind by focusing on their lifestyle while hiding ours. Who are we trying to promote anyway, our gracious God or our holy lifestyles? We must risk rejection by being transparent in order to have miracle-working power. We cannot settle for soulish power, which can build big churches but not powerful Christians.

The Surprise

One day my pastor preached on the cost of revival. As he was speaking he asked us to consider what revival would cost us. At the altar afterwards, I saw a door in my mind's eye. I knew if I opened it the door would reveal the cost of revival for my life. A great fear came over me, because the devil had already told me he would kill my children if I pursued God's anointing any further.

My hand shook as I reached to open that door. I was petrified I would see my children standing there, but I knew I had to move forward. I wanted to obey God, no matter the cost. When I opened the door I saw myself standing there. God told me that my children were safe, but revival would cost me my reputation.

Several months later, I found myself in the middle of a great controversy concerning the prophetic ministry, to which I believe God has called me.

Prophetic ministry is very controversial. A three year battle caused even dear friends to believe horrible things about me. People thought that I was into witchcraft and fortune telling, which is Satan's counterfeit for true prophetic ministry.

I had become an outcast among the churches in my city. The church I was a part of also paid dearly, which was the hardest part for me. Through it all, I had two goals the Lord gave me. First, I was not to defend myself. God wanted to be my Defender. This was hard, because lies were told publicly about me from people I loved and admired. Second, I was not to let the enemy make the people involved my enemy.

God told me we were all being attacked. I was being attacked through rejection and others were being attacked through deception. They were convinced that they were doing the right thing by standing against me. I had to fight to keep my accusers on the same team as me. I knew these people loved God too. I couldn't let the enemy turn them into monsters in my mind. It was one of the hardest things I have ever endured. However, God taught me many things about my gifts and how to use them properly.

I also learned a great deal about other people's gifts and how to minister in unity with them. Although the prophetic ministry is controversial and probably always will be, I know I must obey God, not man. God protected me, He defended me and restored me. Now, I'm not afraid to be rejected or misunderstood, which is inevitable in prophetic ministry. Freedom from the fear of rejection or disapproval comes from embracing rejection not defending ourselves or running from it! Now, that's a surprise!

The struggle with risking rejection is that we all need to feel accepted.

The surprise is when we embrace rejection, God sets us free from ever fearing rejection again.

Let's have a

SoulSOAK

Still your mind • Open your heart • Affirm God's truth • Kindle new passion

The Blessing

Holy Spirit I bless this reader with the desire for truth. I bless them with the freedom to overcome shame and pride. Starting today, they will no longer hide in the shadows. Instead, they will embrace the light of God's truth. They will risk rejection in order to be honest and real with others.

The Meditation

1. Am I afraid for people to discover my weaknesses? If so why? If not, how do I know I am free from this fear?

2. Holy Spirit show me how to living life more transparent without fearing rejection? What can I do to start today?

The Prayer

Jesus I need you to...

9 Arrayed in Armor

When it comes to spiritual warfare, we must be aware of our enemy but not preoccupied with him.

So often when we talk about spiritual warfare the focus is on demonic powers. However, this chapter is going to focus on the winners not the losers. We are on the winning side as believers in Christ. Therefore, this chapter will focus on our Commander-in-Chief, Jesus Christ, and His strategy for war.

I believe that many Christians have their heads in the sand when it comes to spiritual warfare. They think ignorance is bliss and, "if I do not acknowledge Satan, he cannot hurt me." Often, those who are uninformed are critical toward those who are on alert as the Bible commands us to be. The criticism is that the focus is too much on Satan. The fact is, they are probably correct in many cases, but that does not make their position any more right. We must be alert, but not preoccupied.

Be of sober spirit, be on the alert. Your adversary, the devil, prowls about like a roaring lion, seeking someone to devour. But resist him, firm in the faith, knowing that the same experiences of suffering are being accomplished by your brethren who are in the world.

I Peter 5:8, 9 NASB

This passage points out Jesus' strategy for warfare.

1. Be sober, be alert.

The word "sober" in the Greek is "sophroneo." It means to think clearly, to use sound judgment and prudence. The word "alert" is translated as "watchful," or "vigilant." Jesus expects His believers to anticipate and understand the strategy of Satan. We are to be completely aware of who is the enemy and how he works.

The first rule of any war is know your enemy. In Ephesians 6:10-12, Paul cautions us to have our armor on and to stand firm against the enemy. Then he tells us that we do not wrestle against flesh and blood but against principalities and all sorts of demonic powers. Why does he need to clarify who the enemy is? Probably because Christians often do not recognize the real enemy, so they fight with each other instead.

In the chapter on rejection, I shared how the Lord told me not to make enemies out of the Christians who were against me. If God had not made me alert, I probably would have fought against the people accusing me and made things worse. The same principle applies in our homes. How often do we fall for the enemy's plan to steal our joy by causing us to argue with someone right before church?

Many Christians are easily convinced to stay home because they are fixed on people, not God. We must be alert. We must be able to recognize when the enemy has shown up on the scene. If we fail to understand this strategy the devil will defeat us every time. "Be sober, be alert." This is the first strategy of our Commander-in-Chief.

2. *Your adversary...*

As Christians we are not automatically immune from Satan even though he no longer has a legal right to us. It is true that the blood of Jesus has redeemed us from the curse of sin. However, the devil does not care about our rights. In other words, he does not play fair. If we fail to understand his limits, if we fail to exercise our authority over him, he will do whatever we allow him to do. That is what makes him our enemy. That is why there are so many scriptures urging the Christian to resist the devil.

The fact is, the devil has no right to us if we are Christians, but that does not mean anything to him. Since when does the devil follow the rules? God gave man dominion over the earth (see Genesis 1:28). The authority to stop the devil has been given to Christians (see Luke 10:19).

The power to stop him is through the blood (see Colossians 2:15). That is why Revelation 12:11 tells us that we overcome the devil through the word of our testimony and the blood of the lamb. The second strategy of our Commander-in-Chief is to give us the authority over our adversary.

3. The devil prowls about like a roaring lion.

There is significance in understanding this analogy. A roaring lion is an old, tired lion. They roar to paralyze their prey with fear, because they lack the power to destroy them otherwise. A strong, young lion sneaks up and pounces right on his prey with great force and confidence. Not so with a roaring lion. His power is in his roar, not his bite.

The same is true for our enemy. We must not allow him to paralyze us with fear. When we have the presence of God in our lives, we become intimidating to our enemy, which is why he uses fear to paralyze us. If we wise up, we will soon discover just how powerless the devil is against the blood of Jesus.

The fact is the devil has no right to us as Christians but that doesn't mean anything to him. Since when does he follow the rules?

Consider II Corinthians 12:7-12. God tolerated a demon working in Paul's life because He was using that demon to produce humility in Paul. God did the same thing in the strategy of the cross. He let Satan think he had won by giving him a certain amount of power over Jesus. But in the end Satan played right into God's plan. He was using Satan to accomplish His own goals. God does the same thing in our lives. God is still in control.

If we trust Him and understand His strategy, Satan's tricks will play right into God's plans! Now that is power. God is not afraid of Satan. The life of Job demonstrates this strategy. The devil demanded the right to attack Job and God let him do it. "Greater is He that is in us than he that is in the world" (I John 4:4). It is the strategy of our Commander-in-Chief to accomplish His goals in our lives by using the enemy when need be. Therefore, we do not have to fear Satan. We just need to be aware of him.

4. Resist him, standing firm in the faith.

This phrase does not say we will easily defeat the enemy. It says we must keep on standing firm in the faith. Many Christians give up too soon. They allow the enemy to roar too loudly. Spiritual warfare is more about our relationship with God than about the attacks of the enemy.

God wants to produce desperation in us by delaying the answers a bit. Why? Because it is human nature to get overly confident if things come too easily. God is only trying to protect us from ourselves. If things come too easily we start to lose sight of our need for God. Instead, we build our own towers of Babel, thinking we have found some formula for getting what we want from God (see Genesis 11:1-9). This is dangerous thinking! God will not allow us to fall into this pit. That is why Ephesians warns us, "When you have done all you can do to stand, then stand."

So, if you are standing but nothing is happening, do not focus on the devil. Find out what God is up to. You will probably find a weakness God is trying to protect you from, just like Paul did. It is the strategy of our Commander-in-Chief to allow us to keep standing against the devil. If we understand this strategy we will not give up too soon.

5. ...you know that your brothers throughout the world are undergoing the same kind of suffering.

According to this passage in I Peter, our suffering is directly related to the sufferings of the whole church. When one Christian suffers the whole church suffers. The scriptures refer to Christians as the body of Christ (see I Corinthians 12:12-31). Even though we are spread out across the planet, we are still one body. Comparing the church to a single organism helps us to understand one of the most important war strategies of our commander, Jesus Christ.

Just like in the physical body, one part of the body affects the other. If I have a paper cut, my whole hand will feel the effects of that small injury. In the same way, what I go through as a Christian can effect my local church, my city, and even the Kingdom. God designed the church to be interdependent with each other. I cannot accomplish the will of God alone. For instance, my parents could have drastically affected my future if they had not obeyed the Lord. In the same way, if I do not obey the Lord I could have a negative affect on the people of my church.

God is far more confident in His power in us than in Satan's power against us.

This strategy of the Lord's is not designed to put us on a guilt trip. On the contrary, it is meant to protect us. Did you ever notice that the Armor of God listed in Ephesians 6 does not have protection for the back of the solider? The solider of God is to be offensive not defensive. Never turn your back on the devil. Never run away from him. Many Christians are running away from things they are afraid to face. Do not run. Turn around. Face those haunting fears lurking in the background of your thoughts. The truth will set you free (see John 8:32).

Being on the defensive will leave you unguarded. Another reason for this missing piece of armor is that we are to watch each other's back. If you want to get serious about your walk with God, ask a trusted Christian friend to tell you what they see in you. If you're courageous enough to hear the truth, you will be better for it and your relationship with the friend will be unbreakable. God has designed us to be needed. A bond is formed when we show people we need them. This is especially true for leaders. If you want to develop a loyal ministry team, be humble enough to depend on them. Many leaders try so hard to demonstrate how much they know, thinking this will build confidence in the ministry team. It will, but do not be surprised if they leave you, confident that you can do it without them! It is a strategy of our Commander-in-Chief to keep us dependent on each other.

It is the strategy of our Commander-in-Chief to allow us to keep standing against the devil. If we understand this strategy, we will not give up too soon.

6. Focus your attention.

If we focus our attention on the five warfare strategies of God pointed out in I Peter 5:8, then we will surely be equipped to handle whatever battles come our way.

The Struggle

Now that we have a clearer understanding of what spiritual warfare is about, let us consider how we engage these principles we have discussed.

How do we discern when we are under attack? It is dangerous to assume that if things are bad we are being attacked by the devil. I have learned there are three things we need to consider first before we assume we are under attack by the enemy. **First, we may be reaping what we have sown** (see Galatians 6:7) as we have mentioned in a previous chapter. In that case, we need to repent; not war against the Devil.

The law of reaping and sowing does not happen as neatly as some may think. For instance, if you steal from the government by not paying taxes, it doesn't mean you will have money stolen from you. Instead, you may have your authority stolen by having a rebellious child. Most people overlook the law of the harvest as a reason for trials simply because we so easily excuse our sin.

Secondly, like in the case of Job, God can be the reason for the trial. In this case we must submit to God and ask if there is a lesson to be learned. **HINT**: there usually is! If God is trying to teach us something we will keep going through the trial until we get it right. So, if you keep going through the same "stuff," it is best to find out what God wants or you'll be back again.

See, I have refined you, though not as silver; I have tested you in the furnace of affliction. For my own sake, for my own sake, I do this.

Isaiah 48:10, 11a

Thirdly, trials are often designed to give us the opportunity to see the spiritual growth in our lives. When we go through a trial we often recognize things that have changed. I'll give you an example. My personality is not given to detail. This is a quality that the Holy Spirit has been helping me to develop. Every time the golf season starts I have an opportunity to see just how much I have improved in this area of my life. If you play golf you understand what I mean.

When I first started playing I would get so frustrated. My husband would tell me, "Good golfers develop a pre-shot routine." This is a set of rituals designed to control the golfer's swing. Well, I did not have time for that. I would usually quit by the third hole and just follow my husband around as I murmured to myself. Now I have my own pre-swing routine, as well as other routines designed to make my life easier. You may think this is no big deal but that's probably because you have a temperament more like my husband's.

Details and routine are comforting to some and restrictive to others. If God is at work in your life you will see similar challenges; areas of your life that the Spirit of God is transforming. Trials come to show us how we have improved in these areas.

In this you greatly rejoice, though now for a little while you may have had to suffer grief in all kinds of trials. These have come so that your faith…may be proved genuine...

I Peter 1:6, 7

We must consider these three options first in deciding if we are to engage in battle with the devil. If we do not consider these things we will find our selves in a battle we cannot win. We will be fighting the Lord!

If we have determined that we are under attack, how do we fight? The scriptures teach us to covet the spiritual gifts (I Corinthians 14:1). Many Christians struggle with the spiritual gifts because they think they are only used in a public worship service. However, most of the gifts operate in much more practical ways. The spiritual gifts are crucial to our success in spiritual warfare. I could devote a whole chapter to answering this question. Maybe the gifts will be the subject of my next book! For now, let us consider only a few important points.

1. The "discerning of spirits" is different from discernment. The spiritual gift in I Corinthians 12 is "the discerning of spirits." This is the ability to see the spirit at work behind the scenes. It could be the Holy Spirit, a demon or the spirit of man. However, many Christians think they have discernment because they are sensitive to the actions of others. This is often the result be being critical, not gifted.

2. A word of wisdom is often mistaken for discernment. I have heard Christians say that they have good discernment because they are able to make good decisions. This is not the gift of "discerning of spirits," but the gift of a word of wisdom. Wisdom is the ability to properly apply knowledge. This is one of the most useful gifts yet it is rarely recognized as a gift because we take wisdom for granted. Solomon asked for nothing less than wisdom (see II Chronicles 1:10). It was more important to him than all his riches.

3. Speaking in tongues as a prayer language is very useful in spiritual warfare. Often we are unable to understand cognitively what is happening. It is too much for our finite minds to conceive. So when God isn't speaking, it may be that He has too much to say. Use your prayer language during these times.

There is so much more that could be said on this subject. I hope that I have spurred you on to further study the spiritual gifts. I pray that you will covet them, as we are urged to do. The gifts are essential in battle against our enemy. It is also important that we understand demon spirits and their effects on people. However, we must not become preoccupied with this subject.

I urge you to spend at least twice as much time studying the spirit of God as you do in understanding demons. I also urge you to pray twice as much for God to work as you do against Satan from working. Though I believe it is important to learn to fight, the goal is to get to the place of immunity. This is a level of intimacy with God where we are no longer concerned over demons. At this level, demon activity is common, but not feared. God is using you to deal with it appropriately.

However, until we engage in the battle, our disinterest can be mere complacency and our lack of concern naiveté. We must first allow God to expose us to all that we are up against. He can then prepare a table before us in the presence of our enemies (see Psalm 23). Until we know what the enemy is capable of, we cannot fully appreciate what God is doing for us.

Let me give a word of encouragement to the leaders. When you see individuals in your church getting all hyped up about deliverance ministry, do not squelch their zeal or cause them to question what God is showing them. Instead, guide them through this process. Do not operate out of fear but rather grace, and God will bring them to the next stage of their walk. The glory realm is the place of rest, but you cannot rest until you have fought. If you think you are at rest because you have not engaged in spiritual warfare, you are merely ignorant! According to scripture

You cannot rest until you have fought. If you think that you are at rest because you have not engaged in spiritual warfare, you are merely ignorant.

casting out demons is one of the identifying marks of the kingdom of God (Matthew 10:7, 8)! We need to ask, "When was the last time I cast out a demon," before getting critical of those who are at least trying.

We must admit that the church is not winning the battle against the devil yet. I think it is time we go to war. I know that some of these more controversial subjects concerning spiritual warfare have been the center of great disunity. Therefore, let me point out yet another war strategy of our commander, Jesus. Love conquers sin and blessing is greater than cursing. If we bless one another and love each other in spite of our differences God will take care of the things that concern us most.

Submit yourselves, then, to God. Resist the devil, and he will flee from you.

James 4:7

We must stay focused on Jesus our commander in chief. Be aware of the enemy, but not preoccupied with Him. Make it your goal to get to the place of rest, but fight until you get there.

The Surprise

The great surprise of spiritual warfare is that God is always doing a lot more in us than through us. In fact, the reason we have spiritual warfare at all, is so that God can demonstrate His power. When we are aware of something demonic, it is because Satan shows up where God is working.

Surely the sovereign Lord does nothing without revealing his plan to His servants the prophets.

Amos 3:7

God desires to reveal his plan to us. This is the great privilege and responsibility of spiritual warfare. If we focus on God and allow him to show us what he is doing, our perspective will begin to change. We will be able to see the spirit world without reacting to it. God will bring a peace and a rest. I have seen intercessors struggle when this change takes place, thinking that they are losing their passion for God.

Once your eyes are opened, you will not return to inactivity, as long as you stay in right relationship with the Lord. Your activity will focus more on worship and proclamation, rather than warring. This is the beginning of the bride's adornment. As you move deeper in God you will no longer be just a warrior.

You will become the warrior bride!

The struggle with spiritual warfare is learning to stay focused on God when the fight gets intense. We must be aware of Satan but not preoccupied with him.

The surprise of spiritual warfare is that God is always doing more in us than through us. We must make it our goal to get to the place of rest.

We are to become the warrior bride.

Notes

More Notes

10

Kin to the Kingdom

We must see beyond the natural world to see the supernatural. We must see beyond the church to see the kingdom.

The natural and supernatural worlds operate in parallel dimensions. Both worlds are affecting each other, whether we are aware of it or not.

I will give you the keys to the kingdom of heaven; whatever you bind on earth will be bound in heaven, and whatever you loose on earth will be loosed in heaven.

Matthew 16:19

There has been much debate concerning the level of authority this passage is conveying. We will not attempt to figure that out in this book. However, the basic principle of two worlds operating parallel to on another is definitely established here. What we do in the natural world affects what happens in the spiritual world.

When we understand that our obedience or disobedience affects the supernatural world around us then we are becoming kin to the kingdom.

In Daniel chapter 10, the angel of the Lord tells Daniel that he was delayed in coming to him because of the warfare going on in the spirit world. So, not only does our world affect the spirit world, but the spirit world affects our world as well. This is why people are often instructed by God to do something in the natural before God will do something in the super natural.

A Biblical example of this is the walls of Jericho (Joshua 6). Israel had to walk around the walls and then blow the trumpet before God would bring the walls down. Notice that Israel had no understanding as to why they were walking, only that they had to do so for God to intervene. Also, God did not require them to fire weapons or do something else that would apply to their situation.

There are many examples in scriptures of these parallel worlds working together, such as Jesus putting clay on a blind man's eyes so the Father would open them (John 9:5-7). Often what we are required to do does not seem to mean anything in the natural until God does what He does in the supernatural. When we understand that our obedience or disobedience affects the supernatural world around us, then we are becoming a Kin of the Kingdom. Would the walls of Jericho come down if Israel had not walked first? Would the blind man's eyes have opened if Jesus had not put clay on them? Are we willing to do what the Spirit commands, even if it does not seem to be significant or relevant?

Several years ago the Lord instructed me to go to a specific place in our community park which overlooked the downtown area of our city. Once there, I received a word of prophecy that God would bring a spirit of unity to our city. Several weeks later in a prayer meeting, a prophecy came forth that said, "The spirit of unity will be released to dance across our city and remove the strongholds of the enemy."

The next day I made a phone call to an intercessor from another church. They had their weekly prayer meeting at the

Once worship is no longer subjective, but strategic, the heart of the kingdom can be revealed.

same time as we did. I began to share with her the prophecy the Lord had given us during our prayer time. She then shared with me that God had lead her to have all the intercessors at their prayer meeting dance across a map of our city! They were not given the reason for doing this until they heard the prophecy given to us.

Within a year's time twelve organized crime leaders in our city were arrested and put in jail. As a result, roadways and bridges began to get fixed because the money was no longer tied up in crime. The broken down infrastructure of our city has been a huge hindrance for economic growth. In addition, huge strides were made among the spiritual leadership of our city that have begun to bring down the walls of racism and denominationalism. What we do in the natural affects what happens in the supernatural, and the supernatural affects the natural. If we are going to be kin to the kingdom, we must understand this principle.

We must see how God is using us to affect our community and church at large. It is not about growing big churches, but about growing strong Christians.

The Struggle

To be kingdom-minded requires us to look beyond the natural world and beyond the church. We must be more concerned with building the kingdom than building the church. We must be more concerned with pleasing God than pleasing man.

For many years I did the majority of pastoral counseling at my home church. I loved to do it, plus it freed our senior pastor to preach what God instructed without people thinking he was addressing their personal problems publicly. It was a great arrangement.

However, one constant problem continued to exist. Wounded people flooded our church for inner healing, and marriage counseling and other needs. Yet once they were healed they would move on to another church to be leaders. I felt so defeated—why couldn't I benefit from the fruit of my labor? Why wasn't my church benefiting? Just about the time these people could give back to our church, they would leave to bless another church instead. I went to God with this and He began to lift my vision higher. Our church was doing something much greater than building a congregation. We were building the city. God was using us to prepare our community for revival. I knew I needed to give unconditionally and not to expect what I did to benefit only myself or my church.

Over the years I struggled with this concept in several different ways. First, in the area of worship, God began to ask me to dance. I fought this for two reasons. One, I am slightly overweight! Secondly, I was a pastor and thought I needed to keep my dignity. Both of these reasons were rooted in pride!

Contrary to popular opinion, worship is not to be expressed according to our own preferences. The book of Psalms is very specific about God's preferences concerning worship. We are instructed to shout, dance, clap our hands, use the high sounding cymbals and many other instruments. The psalmist does not make these things optional; nor are they reserved for only those whose personalities "are like that." Worship is one of the most basic ways God causes the natural and the supernatural to come together. Remember Jericho—they worshipped and the walls came down.

Worship is more than singing in a church service; it is our life before God. However, corporate worship flows from our life of worship. Worship is not to be subjective, but strategic. The worship leader should be seen as the general in command of an army. When the worship leader instructs us to do certain things during a worship service, such as clap our hands or come to the altar, we need to obey without taking into consideration our own preferences.

God will use our worship as warfare when we understand worship as strategic, not subjective. Of course there are times for personal introspection, but we must develop sensitivity toward the spirit so that we can discern when the spirit is moving strategically in our worship.

For where two or three come together in my name, there I am with them.

Matthew 18:20

If God is in our midst in a corporate setting, He must be in charge. He needs to be leading our worship—not us. Once worship is no longer subjective, but strategic, the heart of the kingdom can be revealed. Developing a kingdom mentality in worship is essential in becoming a kin to the kingdom.

A second area I struggled with in becoming kingdom-minded was in the area of church growth. For a long time I saw the growth of my local church as the proof of faithful ministry. God was not allowing my church to grow like I wanted it to, so apparently the leadership, which included me, was doing something wrong. This is a very narrow and carnal approach. I was definitely church-minded, not kingdom-minded. For instance, when the church outgrew the small building we were in, we sold it. Now, we were getting somewhere, I thought. Then, it took us two years to find property and another two years to build. We were nomads without a place to call our own for more than four years.

Why had God forsaken us like Israel in the wilderness? Surely we had lacked the faith to enter the promised land. Well, God started to show me that he had a purpose in our wanderings that had nothing to do with failure or lack of faith. The middle school in which we first met was in a state of emergency because of its poor grades and lack of good leadership. After two years of prayer and worship in that public school it was voted the number one middle school in our state. God was using this little church to accomplish big things.

The middle school was also located next to the large Catholic church in our community. The community is very religious and not very open to the gospel. It was amazing to see these people standing in the parking lot, week after week, just listening to our worship. We even had a few families come inside one Sunday, and they never returned to their Catholic church. The big breakthrough came, however, when this very closed Catholic church started an ecumenical luncheon and invited all the pastors of our community to share for five minutes about their church and what God was doing there!

Reconciliation will happen when we all realize no church is all right and not church is all wrong. To be kin of the kingdom we must see ourselves as only a part, not the whole.

If you come from a religious community you know the magnitude of that breakthrough. To be kingdom-minded we must be able to see how God is using us to affect our community and church at large. It's not about growing big churches, but about growing strong Christians. It's not about programs but prayer. It's not about what is happening in your church, but what God is doing through your church. During the time our church was without a home, God used us in every location He guided us to. We were a part of breaking down strongholds that have existed in our community for years.

In Numbers 36:5-7, Moses tells the women of Israel that they are only allowed to marry with in their own tribes. Moses told them to do this because God wanted them to maintain their distinctions. When I read this passage I realized that God has always given his people distinctions from the Tower of Babble to the denominations of today. Why has God allowed these differences? He tells us why in Genesis, when He developed the language barrier. It is because humanity is too prideful and will seek to control everything if completely the same.

I no longer believe that what God is doing takes place in a local church. Instead, I believe each church in a community has its own distinction and responsibility. Together we accomplish what God has designed for that city. We must be kingdom-minded, not church-minded, to reach our cities.

Reconciliation is not about overlooking our differences and pretending we see eye to eye. Reconciliation will happen when we realize that no church is totally right and no church is totally wrong. Instead, we all have a piece of the puzzle that needs to be put together with all the other pieces of the puzzle. We can then accept our differences without the need to see eye to eye.

To be a kin of the kingdom we must see ourselves as only a part, not the whole. We must know our part and do it. Then we must link together with the other parts. For instance, it could be interpreted that the Pentecostals are the worshippers, the Baptists are the evangelists, the Catholic are the reverent, the Methodists are the teachers, and so forth. Each distinction can make it hard to accept the other perspectives. However, when grace is added to the mix, nobody has to be proven wrong or right. We all just need to do what God calls us to do and do it well. Together we will get it right!

But in fact God has arranged the parts in the body, everyone of them, just as He wanted them to be. If they were all one part, where would the body be? As it is there are many parts but one body.

I Corinthians 12:18, 20, 21

According to this passage, God has placed us in the body of Christ where He wants us. It is not theological error, but God, who has given us a distinction or specific function in the body. I need to do what I am to do and let everyone else do the same.

To be a kin of the kingdom, we must see beyond the natural world into the supernatural, and see beyond the church into the kingdom.

Let's have a

The Blessing

Lord, I thank you that you have placed this reader exactly where you need them to be. I thank you that you have gifted them with everything they need to accomplish their part in the kingdom of God. I know You want them to do their part so You can do your part. I proclaim Your purposes to be fulfilled in them. They will be free from doctrinal debates. Instead, they will embrace what You are doing in others and allow Your grace to govern their relationships in the kingdom.

The Meditation

1. What keeps me from understanding the spirit world around me better? Is it fear, pride, logic or something else standing in my way?

2. Do I know my part in the body? Am I doing it?

The Prayer

Lord, I know the scripture teaches that the spirit world exists. I know that I am to walk by faith and not by sight. Yet to walk by sight seems easier at times; there is less risk, less faith too. Help me to obey You when the Spirit tells me something that my natural mind wants to reject.

If I am going to be kingdom- minded I must know my part in the body and do it. So, Lord help me to...

The Surprise

When the Holy Spirit begins to enlarge our scope of understanding, God becomes amazingly strong and so much bigger than we allowed Him to be. God is not worried about doctrinal errors and theological debates. He is after the heart of man; not our intellect. For instance, the first time God lead my church to have a Super Bowl party instead of Sunday night service, we took a lot of heat for it. Several pastors in the area rebuked our church from their pulpit without mentioning our name. They told their congregations that, "Real Christians are in church on Sunday night."

God is always in control. He may only appear to need our help because of our small understanding of Him.

Paul told us the real church becomes all things to all men so that by all possible means we might save some (see I Corinthians 9:22). That night at the Super Bowl party, someone was baptized in the Holy Spirit during half time. Since then, the Super Bowl party has been one of our most effective outreaches. We have seen many young people enter our church doors for a party that would have never come for a church service. We must allow God to enlarge our scope of understanding. He is so much more creative than for what we give Him credit. Church, to God, is not a building or a scheduled event. Whenever Christians come together that's church, no matter what we are doing. Developing this mentality gives the Holy Spirit the opportunity to use us wherever we are.

Several years ago on New Year's Eve, a group of my Christian friends and I went out to eat at a restaurant. Sitting across from us was a group of punk rockers. The Holy Spirit told me to go talk to them about Christ. When I asked for someone to go with me, they all laughed at me. When I approached the table, I asked if I could talk to them for a minute. The whole restaurant went silent. I began to share the gospel with them and discovered they were a Christian punk rock group that had just come from a youth service.

I knew then that God had asked me to go over to that table to teach something to all the Christians in the room. Now, whenever I go into a public place I tell myself "let the church service begin!" Sometimes I get to preach, sometimes I do not, but I am always prepared to have church even when it's not a Sunday night.

When I was in Bible College one of my professors used to give me the same advice each time I sought her council. She would say two things to me, "The kingdom of God is bigger than that," and "The journey is the destiny." At the time these two statements were so much bigger than my understanding that I found them trite. But over the years I have grown into them.

First, the kingdom of God is so much bigger than what we know. We should never be so certain we understand. God is always in control. He may only appear to need our help because of our small understanding.

Secondly, God is far more concerned with who we are and what we are learning than where we are going. We should not be so focused on the future that we lose sight of the present. God is at work in our day to day lives and it is His desire that we meet Him there. Take time to enjoy the process; that is where you will find the joy of the Lord.

> *If the Lord delights in a man's way, He makes his steps firm; though he stumble, he will not fall, for the Lord upholds him with his hand.*
>
> *Psalm 37:23*

We struggle to be kingdom-minded when it is hard to see beyond the natural into the supernatural, and when it is hard to see beyond the church into the kingdom.

It is a surprise to discover that the kingdom of God really is bigger than the things that concern us. It is a comfort to know God really is in control and does not need our help, He chooses it.

Notes

More Notes

11

Grasping God's Glory

Experiencing the Glory of God is like coming face to face with a powerful lion only to see the gentleness in his eyes.

God's glory is a paradox. It is both terrifying and comforting at the same time. There is a great sense of awe that makes you want to bow. There is a deep sense of love and acceptance that cradles you like a newborn child in the arms of a loving mother. God's presence is both authority and love working together; the two great powers of the universe entrusted to mankind. From the human race emerges male and female: authority and love personified. Oh, that we could understand each other in the unity of God himself. We are a reflection of Him after all, created in His image. We are the glory of God on the earth.

"He raises the poor from the dust and lifts the needy from the ash heap; He seats them with princes and has them inherit a throne of honor"

I Samuel 2:8

God fills my heart with wonder and amazement every time I consider His love for me. Why does he love and honor us so? We are totally undeserving and could never be His equal, yet He treats us as though we are. Amazing—absolutely amazing!

What is the glory of God?

The Vine's Expository Dictionary defines the Glory of God as the divine splendor and perfection in self-manifestation. In other words, everything that God is, made known to us. God wants us to experience Him. He does not want to be a theological belief or an opinion we regard defensively. God wants us to see, feel, touch, embrace and understand everything about him. God desires intimacy with humanity. He wants us to be his bride.

My prayer as I pen this book is that somehow a passion to know God is imparted to you. I pray that this book will leave a craving for God so big in your heart that you will stop at nothing and will be willing to give up everything just to have it satisfied. We must grasp the glory of God. We must have the splendor of Him made real to us.

The Struggle

Let me warn you. This kind of passion for God is both exhilarating and terrifying. The desire has become so big for me that very little satisfies it. No matter what God does, I still want more. I know that I have not even begun to know Him, for He is eternal. He is limitless. He is omniscient.

Because of this, there is a struggle between passion and patience, between expectation and contentment, between hope and thankfulness.

Have you ever wanted something so badly that you were miserable waiting for it. I get like that sometimes. I just want to see God get the recognition He deserves. So, I get frustrated with the people around me that take Him for granted. I want to see people worshiping God according to His beauty not their comfort zone. I want to see God show up like He did in the Old Testament. Maybe if He parts another sea we'll get it! But Israel didn't get it. Instead, they made a golden calf and worshipped a hunk of metal!

So, what is the solution? How do we have passion and contentment at the same time? How can we be passionate to see the purposes of God fulfilled and rest in His presence at the same time?

Let us, therefore, make every effort to enter that rest...

Hebrews 4:11

According to this passage it will require effort to enter into God's rest. We can not skip over the effort and go straight to the resting part or we may end up in complacency. Let me tell you my cracker story. Several years ago my husband and I were on a much needed weekend getaway. As we were traveling in the car, I was rambling on about how much I wanted to see God move in our church. We had been praying fervently for years yet in my estimation, not enough was happening. Well, my husband is a patient man, but I pushed him over the edge that day. He yelled at me!

"You're never satisfied, are you? Why can't you be thankful for what is happening instead of frustrated about what isn't?" A word to those of us with prophetic giftings, this is the weakness we bear. We live so much in the future that we are discontent in the present. Prophetic people are often angry people; we need the Lord to help us with that.

So, back to the story. I looked at my husband with tears running down my cheeks and said, "I feel like a beggar coming out of the desert. God is there to help me, but He only gives me a cracker and expects me to be thankful. I am thankful, but I am still very hungry and very thirsty!"

With that, we sat in silence and a great heaviness for several minutes. Then all of a sudden, as we turned a corner it appeared right it front of us... We were headed straight toward the Nabisco Cracker Factory. There were huge silos many stories high and a big sign that read, "Home of the Cracker."

Rest is the result of grasping God's glory. When we see Him manifested in all His splendor we will rest from our labors.

My husband and I started laughing so hard, and we laughed for miles. I'm still laughing about the goodness of God as I sit at my computer telling you this story. It was as if God was saying, "I may only give you one cracker at a time, but look at all the crackers I have."

Patience is the ability to keep your passions at a distance. Gentleness is the ability to have power over your powers. It is like holding a small bird in your hand even though you could crush it. It will require the fruit of patience and gentleness to bring a balance between our passion for God's glory and His rest. We must have rest. The ability to rest in God is the goal He is trying to achieve in each of our hearts (see Matthew 11:28). ***Rest is the result of grasping God's glory.*** For when we see him manifested in all His splendor we become confident in God's wisdom and abilities; we abandon all our own efforts (Hebrews 4:10). We will see things as He sees them. It is no longer about trying to do God's work but believing God to do His work through us.

Write down the revelation and make it plain on tablets so that a herald may run with it. For the revelation awaits an appointed time; it speaks of the end and will not prove false. Though it linger, wait for it; it will certainly come and will not delay.

Habakkuk 2:2, 3

"Though it linger, wait for it"... it will not delay." There is a great tension between these words; it lingers but does not delay. Only those who are at rest in God can live comfortably in this tension. We must passionately believe and patiently wait at the same time. I wish I could tell you that I have achieved this rest completely. However, I am learning the difference between living for faith and living by faith.

To live for faith requires activity. I have something to prove and I must meet the expectations of those around me. To live for faith requires me to look up to the throne crying out for God to move. To live by faith is a place of rest. There is nothing to prove because only God's opinion matters. Instead, of looking up to the throne we will look down from it. We see what God sees and so there is only proclamation. This is a totally different place to be in God. It is the goal of God and our privilege to come to this place of rest (see Psalm 91:1-2).

The subject of divine healing is a good example of this tension. I am required to believe God will heal people and to pray in faith that they will be. Yet if divine healing does not happen, I cannot let this stop me from believing for the next person. I must passionately believe and patiently wait! How? My faith must be in God and not my faith. I have to do my job with no concern for results. The results are God's responsibility and the faith is mine. Many of the names that are listed in the hall of faith (Hebrews 11) are there because they believed, even though they did not see the promise fulfilled in their lifetime. It will come and our faith is a part of bringing it to pass. However, we may not get to see it ourselves.

Several years ago I saw a movie that best illustrates this point. The movie was about the development of the western frontier. The story line followed the lives of two women who talked their families into giving up everything to move out west, before the "west" was developed. At the end of the movie the two women were standing alone in a homemade cemetery surrounded by the graves of their entire family. They felt defeated and lost. They were mourning their decision as they turned to walk away. As they faded into the field of undeveloped land, I was overwhelmed by the strength and faith upon which our great country is built.

Many people in those days never lived to see their own fortune or dreams come true. However, we have them to thank for ours! In the same way, we may not see every person healed when we pray, but our faith will make a difference nonetheless. That is what it means to see things from the throne. From God's point of view our daily activities are only apart of a much bigger plan. Like the construction of a beautiful puzzle, God adds in each part where it belongs. We must be willing to do our part and leave the rest to God. So, keep believing, keep praying, keep living by faith and never give up knowing your faith is making a difference even if you can not see it with your own eyes. This is how we rest in God.

Keep in mind, this rest comes after we have become the warrior for God. God's rest is very different from carnal rest. Carnal rest is the result of ignorance or complacency. Carnal rest says, "your will be done Lord." There is no passion, no risk, with that kind of rest. Divine rest says, "I believe you will do what you say you will do; even in the face of defeat I will not be moved."

If what you have been reading in this book is new to you, you might feel uneasy and even scared. That is the result of revelation. We are always a little scared when we first see the truth. It is overwhelming to have our eyes open to the majesty of God. He is awesome! Do not run from this fear just keep moving forward and God will give you rest. If our relationship with God is growing we will continually have our eyes opened to see God a little bit bigger than we were able to see Him before. If you have been saved for a while and do not have times when God's greatness is unsettling, then your relationship has grown cold and you need your fire rekindled (see Matthew 24:12).

God wants to live in us… uninterrupted by our own ideas and thoughts. He wants us to be at rest so he can do his work through us. This place of rest is the glory of God being manifested in us.

Many Christians have become complacent and do not realize it. If your understanding of God and how He does things has not changed recently, then you are in danger of complacency. God is infinite we must always be growing in our understanding of who He is (see Ephesians 1:17-19).

To live in God's rest is a subconscious experience. I know when I have walked out of rest because I become conscious of what I am doing. I start asking questions. I start to wonder if I am doing the right things. I am so aware of myself and others. I ask myself questions like, "Is the person I'm praying for being offended or comforted?" Or, I might be concerned that I am too loud in worship. I might make a decision about something and then later start to rethink it. I get uncomfortable and distracted by my own thoughts. But when I am resting in God he has total control of my actions and so I am not aware of myself at all.

When I am at rest I will preach and have an altar call and never once think about myself or the people around me. God just does what He wants to do and I am out of the way entirely. God wants to be able to live in us uninterrupted by our own ideas and thoughts. He wants us to be at rest so he can do his work through us. This place of rest is the glory of God being manifested in us.

The Surprise

This place of rest is challenging to acquire simply because we do not trust that God is the one guiding us. We have a hard time totally expecting God to keep us on the right track. We think there is some responsibility on our part. The will of God becomes a tightrope walk over the flames of hell.

How can we be at rest when we are carrying so much responsibility? It comes as a surprise to realize that this sense of responsibility is a hindrance to God, not an expectation of His. Psalm 37:23 tells us that God holds on to us, we do not hold on to God. We can never truly experience God's keeping power unless we let go and stop trying to keep ourselves. It is kind of like floating. It is the hardest thing to figure out, but once you do, it works no matter how deep the waters.

The Lord is my Shepherd, I shall not be in want. He makes me
lie down in green pastures, he leads me besides still waters...
You prepare a table before me in the presence of my enemies.
You anoint my head with oil; my cup overflows.

Psalm 23:1, 2, 5

This entire Psalm is a beautiful picture of the rest that comes when you see God in his splendor. David was truly captivated by God. His heart trusted in him, because he knew he had failed and yet God loved him. Let me draw your attention to three phrases in this passage.

First, "I shall not want." This is a declaration, not a promise. David was saying, I will not allow my passions to get the best of me, for God is the one leading my life. It does not mean that God is promising to do everything we want him to do. The place of rest requires a choice on our part.

When the church where I served as associate pastor was not growing, many advised me to give up. Books were given to me about church growth. Many stated if a church did not grow within three years, it never would. Yet God was saying, "Hold on. I have a purpose here and I need you to rest in Me." I had to choose to listen to God and be at rest, instead of listening to the advice of others that were telling me to get busy or move on.

Second, 'He makes me." This insinuates that we may not want to do it. Rest is so foreign to our way of thinking. We are very religious people by nature. The focus is usually on us not God. But God will lead us to this place of rest. When God told me to write this book He also told me to resign my positions at the church, give up my salary and move my office home. I was to concentrate on the book only.

This was not easy because our church was in a building project and I wanted to help. I felt it was horrible timing for my church family. I obeyed God and others stepped up to the plate to take my place in the various ministries I headed. My absence created the vacuum God need to promote others in their gifts. When God is leading us to rest we must obey.

Third, "He prepares a table in the presences of my enemies." When I think of a banquet table I visualize a beautiful dinning room with lots of candles and soft music. Who wouldn't want to be invited to that kind of table? But the table in Psalm 23 needs to be visualized on a battlefield with bombs and guns going off all around it.

Imagine being a soldier on the front lines and you get the command to attend a dinner party prepared by the general across the enemy line. How comfortable would you be sitting and relaxing without any weapon in that environment? This is what God wants for us. He wants us to have so much confidence in him that we will allow him to prepare a table in the presence of our enemies.

When God first started to reveal the reality of demonic activity to me I wanted to cast out every demon he showed me. People started inviting me to their homes because they had seen a demon and wanted me to get rid of it for them. I felt like a spiritual superhero, I had come to save the day! Then one day God told me not to get rid of the demon I saw. The Lord was using that demon just like He used the messenger of Satan in Paul's life (II Corinthians 12:7).

I left the home without dealing with the demon. This was a little scary because I thought I should have dealt with the enemy, but God wanted me to put down my weapon and rest. Sometime later the father of that home saw the demon. He then confessed that he thought his wife and I were crazy until he saw it for Himself. Once the head of the Home took authority over that demon it was gone. We must learn to rest, even on the battlefield. It is God's war—not ours.

Arise, shine for your light has come, and the glory of the Lord rises upon you. See, darkness covers the earth and thick darkness the peoples, but the Lord rises upon you and his glory appears over you.

Isaiah 60:1, 2

The struggle to grasp God's glory is in finding the balance between passion and patience.

Once we start to grasp the glory of God we are surprised by the place of rest it brings us to.

The Blessing

We will lie down in the green pastures of God's rest. We will learn to partner with the Holy Spirit to balance passion and patience. We will declare God to be the supplier of all we need.

We will not allow ourselves to feel lack. Instead, we will trust God for what we have and what He allows in our lives.

The Meditation

1. Is the Lord your shepherd, meaning you allow Him to lead you by the quiet streams to lie down in the pastures? Here are a few questions to ask yourself, if you are not sure:

   a. Are you able to sleep at night, even when things are not good at work, or do you lie there trying to work it out in your head?

   b. Are you able to listen patiently to someone's complaints without getting defensive or do you justify yourself with excuses or point out their failures?

   c. When the prayer request you have been believing for delays or does not happen, do you feel abandoned by God or do you trust Him to know something you do not know?

2. God wants you to sit and enjoy a nice dinner on the battlefield of your life. In what area of your life or thoughts are you struggling to stay seated, instead of getting up to fix it?

   Ask the Holy Spirit why and what you must do to be able to rest.

The Prayer

Lord, rest is not always easy for me. At times, I feel it would be irresponsible to doing nothing. Other times, I am too afraid to rest; my mind is filled with the "what if" questions. Yet I know I am probably in your way because of my lack of trust. Teach me to...

Notes

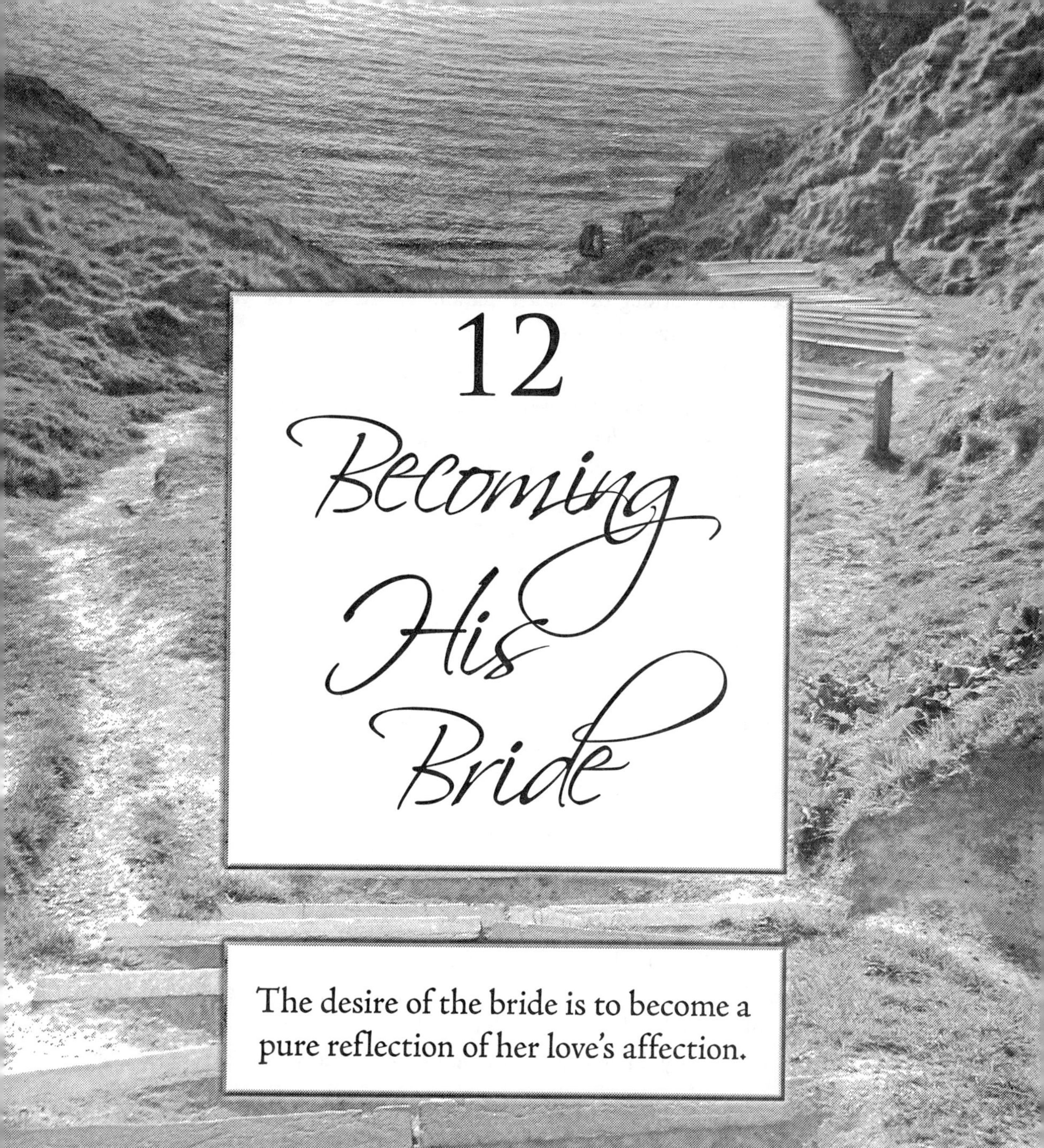

12

Becoming His Bride

The desire of the bride is to become a pure reflection of her love's affection.

Well, this is it. The final stage and hope for every true believer in Jesus Christ. We are to be his bride. We will reign with Jesus as joint heirs of the throne of God. Everything about our life culminates in this one true fact. We have been created for an intimate personal relationship with God because of the Father's love, through our Bridegroom's sacrifice and according to the work of the Holy Spirit in our lives. We are destined for the throne.

But because of His great love for us, God, who is rich in mercy, made us alive with Christ even when we were dead in transgressions - it is by grace you have been saved. And God raised us up with Christ and seated us with Him in heavenly realms in Christ Jesus, in order that in the coming ages He might show the incomparable riches of His grace, expressed in His kindness to us in Christ Jesus.

Ephesians 2:4-6

Many of us understand God as Judge, as Savior, as Warrior King. We have faced His judgments. We have been redeemed by Jesus' shed blood and we have seen His power demonstrated in our lives. Yet, do we know Him as our Bridegroom? Do we understand ourselves to be joint heirs of the throne? Do we live our lives as though we are seated with Christ in heavenly places? Have we become lovers with God?

He is our Bridegroom

I remember my wedding night like it was yesterday. I had never felt so pure, so loved as I did that night. My husband took me in his arms and said, "Well Mrs. Chickonoski I am about to make love to you for the first time." It was incredible. However, the next morning when I had to get out of the bed and let my new husband see me in broad daylight, it was a different story. I tried to quietly tiptoe to the bathroom, but before I got there he turned on the light. I dropped to the floor and screamed. I wasn't ready to be that close.

Many of us live our relationship with the Lord this way. We are afraid to be ourselves, we are afraid to let God see us completely unclothed. We know He sees everything anyway, but somehow it seems better not to admit it openly. At some point, our relationship with Jesus must progress beyond this illusion. If we cannot admit our true feelings to God, how can He heal us? If we are afraid to admit our faults, He can not transform us.

Jesus is the lover of our soul. He will not be disappointed, only compassionate. He will not market our weaknesses and expose us in humiliation. It is Satan who is our accuser. He is the one who brings condemnation upon us. He does this in order to discredit God in our eyes, not the other way around. Satan is smart enough not to try to get God to give up on us. He brings accusation against us so we will give up on God. Think about how you feel when you listen to the accusations. God becomes something less in your mind than he is in the scriptures.

If we cannot admit our true feelings to God, how can he heal us? If we are afraid to admit our faults, how can he transform us?

We think things like, "God can't possibly love me after what I've done," or "God can't use me because I'm..." The power to destroy our relationship with God is not in how our negative thoughts make us feel about ourselves, but in how human they make God appear.

Most of us as parents have probably questioned the wisdom of God in giving us children at one time or another. I remember one time in particular when I said, "God I am going to mess these kids up for sure." The Lord's kind response to me was, "Yep." I realized that even though I was raised by amazing Christian parents they too had passed on undesirable things to me. However, it was in the struggle of those very things that I got to know God better. That day, the Lord showed me He was not dependent upon me for the right things. He would use even the wrong things to help my children, if I just prayed and believed Him to do so. I also, realized that if I beat myself up over the failures, I would do more damage to my children. I had to change the negative thoughts about myself and believe that God was still who He said He was, even when I failed.

For I am convinced that neither death nor life, neither angels nor demons, neither the present nor the future, nor any powers, neither height nor depth, nor anything else in all creation, will be able to separate us from the love of God that is in Christ Jesus our Lord.

Romans 8: 38, 39

How persuaded are you of God's love for you? Do you see Him as your Bridegroom?

The Struggle

Here is the struggle. We do not buy it! It cannot be that easy! The religious part of us comes out and we say, "Come on, God does not wink at sin. He wants us to be holy just like He is holy." You will get no argument from me on that one. However, we will not serve a God we fear more than a God who captivates us by His love. Fear is an inferior motivator to love. If I am convinced of God's love, I will serve Him out of passion, not obligation. Passion will purify me much quicker than obligation.

How great is the love the Father has lavished on us, that we should be called the children of God! And that is what we are!... Everyone who has this hope in him purifies himself, just as He is pure.

I John 3:1, 3

When we become the bride, we must lay down the sword for the scepter.

The scepter is the symbol of royalty and authority. As the queen, we no longer are required to fight. We are now joint heirs. When God started this process in me my attitude began to change about spiritual warfare. I no longer had a passion to fight demons—they were much less of a threat to me. God helped me to see demons in the same way He sees them. They are used by God to accomplish His work.

The power to destroy our relationship with God is not in how our negative thoughts make us feel about ourselves, but in how human they make God appear.

For instance, when revival hit America in the late 1990's, many of the Christians in our town were traveling to Florida for a touch of God. I was on one of the first bus loads. Great things began to take place in our city as a result. However, like any God-ordained revival, there were those taking a stand against what was happening. Some Christians were up in arms defending their position.

God showed me that He was only using the resistance like a pressure cooker. He told me not to come to His defense because I would only look like I was defending myself. I declared God's purposes over the city and waited for God to do what He wanted to do.

Looking back, I believe the Holy Spirit was quenched and what God wanted to do was put on hold, but I believe God let it happen for a reason. He is always in control. When we develop intimacy with Jesus and lay down our sword for the scepter we become privy to information that keeps us at rest.

Remember, if we skip the warrior stage it may not be the scepter that is keeping us out of the battle but our lack of understanding.

The rest and authority of the bride is a reward to the warrior. At first, this authority will feel like the king's armor felt on David (I Samuel 17). We have to grow into it. Here are a few of the changes the scepter will bring into our life:

We no longer carry burdens as though they are our own.

Our prayer life will change drastically. We are no longer warriors fighting on behalf of others. Instead, we are the bride who is carrying her warrior's burden. Imagine Jesus coming home from the battle. As his bride we would comfort him by listening to him share the struggles of his day. It is not our fight. We are safe in the palace. It is our Savior's fight. All we have to do is be the supportive bride. We no longer pray as though we are pleading a case before the throne. Whatever we desire to pray is the burden Jesus is sharing with us. We are carrying His prayers to the throne, not our own. In this way, we have a greater confidence that what we pray for will happen.

Therefore He is able to save completely those who come to God through him, because He always lives intercede for them.

Hebrews 7:25

Our prayer life becomes the comfort of the bride toward her Warrior Bridegroom. Jesus is the victor. He will not lose His battle. We cannot hope for something that God will not do. The woman of Song of Solomon says it best.

I belong to my lover and His desire is for me.

Song of Solomon 7:10

At the beginning of Song of Solomon the woman said, "My lover is mine and I am his" (see 2:16). Here, her own priorities come first—he belongs to me. Then, a little deeper into the relationship, she reverses it, "I am my beloved's and He is mine (see 6:3). She still has her own priorities, but Jesus comes first. The final stage of the bride is when we can say, "I belong to my lover and His desire is for me." Here she has no priorities of her own. She desires only what Jesus desires.

Once we reach this stage of oneness with Jesus we will not have a burden that is our own. Our burdens and hopes are those of our bridegroom. Of course, this kind of confidence is produced through purity and humility, which we receive as we journey from being a disciple to the bride of Christ. There are no shortcuts. There is a price to pay for this kind of authority.

As the bride of Christ we cannot hope for something the bridegroom will not do. Our desires are His.

I realize that the analogy of the supportive bride toward the warrior husband is difficult for a man in which to relate. The relationship of Jonathan and David is probably a better example for men. In I Samuel 18:1-3, the scripture says that Jonathan's spirit was knit to David's and he loved him as himself. The level of commitment between these two men on the battlefield is the same level of intimacy trust and unity that Jesus desires with all Christian men.

In II Samuel 1:26, David says of Jonathan's love that it was better than the love of a woman. This was not a reference to homosexuality, for the law completely forbid it (Leviticus 18:22, 20:13). Instead, I believe David, who had a harem full of women, shared a spiritual and emotional oneness with Jonathan that surpassed even sex! That's amazing that a man would find something he thought better than sex!

So, you can see this kind of emotional intimacy is possible for men. I am sure that Jonathan's strength, loyalty, and friendship on the battlefield was much more appreciated than all David's concubines dancing for him out there. No insult to the strength of women intended; in the Old Testament women had no use in battle. A similar analogy might be the unity and commitment required between to police partners. They need to have each other's back; they cannot afford personal distractions. Their minds need to be clear and completely focused on each other. This is the relationship Jesus is looking for in us.

Your corporate worship becomes an expression of the bridegroom's passionate heart.

Humanity has a heightened sensitivity to pleasure. Even certain parts of our body demonstrate this fact. This sensitivity causes us to become attached to whatever brings us pleasure. God gave us this sensitivity so that we could bond with Him through worship.

> *You have made known to me the path of life; you will fill me with joy in your presence, with eternal pleasures at your right hand.*
>
> ❧ *Psalm 16:11*

Keep in mind that Satan was the worship leader in heaven until he decided he wanted the worship of God for himself. Therefore, Satan will do everything in his power to prevent worship from being pleasurable. He does not want us to experience pleasure in worship so that we will not bond with God. Worship is personal, but it must be expressed among the brethren. When we focus on God and enjoy His presence together, without judgment, we become one. Jesus prays in John 17, "Father make them one even as We are one." The bride understands that worship is an expression of the bridegrooms love for her and she enjoys it!

There is a river whose streams make glad the city of our God.

Psalm 46:4

There does not need to be a bigger theological reason for the manifestations of God in worship than that. It is just plain fun to see God working through the human reactions to His presence! That is God's goal. He wants us to enjoy Him, for when we do, we will have an unbreakable bond with Him. Learn to enjoy God!

As the bride we will develop a desire to share God's glory with others.

There is no longer a need to earn respect when we see ourselves as the bride of Christ. There is a union with our bridegroom that causes us to be totally fulfilled in God alone. When this happens, we will find more joy in seeing others gain honor than ourselves. We will look for the opportunity to promote others in the kingdom, rather than seeking our own recognition. We will be able to do the work and allow someone else to get the credit for it.

And without faith it is impossible to please God, because anyone who comes to Him must believe that He exists and that He rewards those who earnestly seek Him.

Hebrews 11:6

We all have a desire for recognition and reward. It is a human need to be accepted; recognition is one way of achieving acceptance. However, the recognition of heaven is far more superior to that of the world. God does want to reward us, but we must choose which kind of reward will satisfy us. If we crave the inferior recognition of humanity we will lose out on God's reward. Once we discover this truth we will desire only God's recognition.

Over the years I have endured some painful times of rejection, times when my efforts went unnoticed by others and made me feel unappreciated. This was an occurrence that happened frequently, to the point that others began to notice and felt badly for me. It became a joke with my husband and me. Inside it hurt, even though I knew I should not be upset, I was.

The American church has a very shallow concept of suffering. We often interpret "abundant life" as the American dream.

Then one day while talking to a friend God revealed something to me. My friend and I were standing on the back deck of my new home. My husband and I could have never afforded this home except for the miracle of God's provision. I began to share with my friend that I would much rather have this beautiful home than my name in a program or announced from a platform.

At that moment, I realized that God had done me a favor by not allowing me to gain human recognition until His recognition was all I desired. We will desire to share God's glory with others once we see ourselves as the bride.

The Blessing

Say this blessing with me: I am the bride of Christ. I know God enjoys me and I enjoy Him. I will have the loyalty and unity of Jonathan and David in my relationship with Jesus. I declare my allegiance to the King of Kings. I will have no other distractions that would prevent God from accomplishing His plan in and though me.

The Meditation

1. Do you feel like a servant or a friend to Jesus?

2. Do you enjoy God? Do you believe He enjoys you?

3. Do I seek recognition and face jealousy when others prosper or do I desire to promote others and help them succeed?

The Prayer

How I long to be one with you Jesus. I do not want to have my own way. I want to follow yours. I count it a privilege to be able to have relationship with you. Forgive me for the times I have taken it for granted. Lord, I want to...

The bride of Christ must embrace the cross.

The American church has a very shallow concept of suffering. For the most part, we interpret "abundant life" as the "American dream." Many Christians think living a godly life some how obligates God to give them what they want. This philosophy is reinforced by all the "great testimonies" televised and promoted in the Christian media. We have been convinced that life should be totally "successful" for the "really dedicated" Christian.

However, if you read Hebrews 11, which is known as the "Hall of Faith," you will discover something very different than the American dream. Most of the people recognized for their great faith never saw the promises of God fulfilled, yet they still believed God.

It does not take great faith to have all your dreams come true. A little hard work and a positive attitude can give you your dreams. Real faith is developed when we embrace the cross. Jesus appeared foolish, unsuccessful, and defeated to most people in his day and by many still. God defeated the enemy by allowing Jesus to give up everything. This is the price of the cross. We must be willing to give up everything. As the bride of Christ we cannot avoid this pain.

Remember the movie "Spartacus?" Kirk Douglas plays a Roman gladiator that organizes a revolt against the empire. At the end, he is hanging on a cross for his rebellion. At his feet is his wife begging him to die because she can not bear to see him in pain. To me, this is the perfect picture of the bride of Christ, our suffering is for Him. As she is standing there she holds up their new born son. "He is free Spartacus, free," she says. Even though the gladiator dies a gladiator, his son goes free; a perfect picture of Jesus.

We must keep the faith and be willing to suffer for the gospel's sake. We may not see all our dreams come true but we are making others free. We are the bride of Christ and we cannot avoid the suffering of the cross. "For better or for worse;" this is our vow as the bride of Christ. The bride suffers because of her position, not for it. Abundant life is not the American dream. Abundant life is the ability to live with hope and grace in spite of suffering.

He saved us, not because of righteous things we have done, but because of his mercy. He saved us through the washing of rebirth and renewal by the Holy Spirit, whom he poured out on us generously through Jesus Christ our savior, so that, having been justified by his grace, we might become heirs having the hope of eternal life.

Titus 3:5-7

The Surprise

There are three things that I have learned along my personal journey with Jesus Christ that I hold most valuable. I have saved these things for last in the hopes that they are what you will remember most vividly.

First, growing in God means you see the things you have always seen with greater understanding and teach it with greater grace. If you are growing in the love of God the more you understand, and the more understanding you are of others.

Second, growing in God's grace means you learn to say less so God can do more. The more you know, the less you want to say because you do not want to rob God of the opportunity to reveal Himself to others.

Third, growing in faith means you learn to lean on God without the fear of failure or the fear of man. We can risk being wrong and accept the criticism of others with grace because God is the single most important factor in all that we do.

We have discussed many things throughout the pages of this book. The journey will take a lifetime though the words to describe it are few. Of course, this is just a taste of what lies ahead for each of us as we grow in God. The crescendo of our journey is our intimacy with the bridegroom. The greatest surprise we will discover along the way is God himself. He wants us to be united with him. This unity is a continual climax that just keeps taking us to new heights and greater depth. Just when we think our vision has been lifted as high as it can go, there is more to see.

Just when we think we have experienced the depth of God's love and knowledge we are challenged to go deeper. Always higher—always deeper! Never, never give up or give in. The road is exhausting and the path is lonely at times. The enemy is always there trying to distract us so that he can destroy us. Oh, but the joy is immense and the rewards indescribable. The love of God is unquenchable and his pleasures unceasing! Wherever you are in your journey with God remember...

You are becoming lovers with Jesus.

Do not allow anyone or anything to lessen this reality. God is in love with you. He is your pursuer and his love will be as pure and satisfying as your heart will allow. Do not give in to mere humanity, for it will hold you back or cloud your vision. Be a lover of God. Let God become you as you are united with Him through His love.

I want to leave you with these two prayers the Holy spirit gave me. Hold on to them, treasure them and live them.

The Prayer of the Bride

I know now the place of rest is the position and power of the bride.

I make my requests before you my beloved, knowing
you desire to please me, as I do you my Lord.

Cause me to abide in your chambers, to not abandon the place of coheir.

For your blood has granted me the position of
equality though I will never be your equal.

To live in a lesser place is to neglect your great salvation.

Sin is beneath me now as your bride, lack of self control
demeaning and laziness an embarrassment.

I desire to be a pure reflection of my Lord's affection.

May our love be compelling and my life a gift worthy of You my Lord.

The Bridegroom's Response

My dearly beloved, how my heart is full of love for you my bride.

I long to touch your Spirit and hold your dreams close to my heart.

You have filled me with great joy, because of your passion for me
and your determination to live in the land of the living.

I see your heart cannot be quenched; the fire of your love burns stronger with every douse of pain and disappointment the enemy has thrown at you.

Do not fear I am here.

I can no longer wait to lavish my love upon you.

I want to fulfill every dream, make every plan a reality, for your heart is my heart.

You long for what I long for.

As my bride I have adorned you with jewels more precious than those of diamond, emerald, or pearl.

I have adorned you with beauty this world could never behold.

It is too costly for this world to bestow value.

For I have lavished upon you the door of the Kingdom, the authority of the bride, the access into my chambers, the beauty of godly wisdom, the grace of unconditional love and the attraction of humility.

These jewels adorn my bride, you are my bride.

Notes

More Notes

More Notes